John Wyclif

Wycliffe Studies in History,
Church, and Society

GENERAL EDITOR: THOMAS P. POWER

The series aims to draw on historical scholarship from new and established scholars in the
history of Christianity broadly defined. Titles
in the series will be topical but general enough
to be appealing. The subject matter will cover
topics of general interest in the field of Christian history. The goal is to produce short pam-
phlets on historical topics of broad general
interest in an accessible way.

Other Titles in the Series

A Confusion of Printers: *The Role of Print in
the English Reformation*—Pearce J. Carefoote

John Wyclif

New Perspectives on an Old Controversy

BY
Sean A. Otto

WIPF & STOCK · Eugene, Oregon

JOHN WYCLIF
New Perspectives on an Old Controversy

Wipf & Stock
An Imprint of Wipf and Stock Publishers
199 W. 8th Ave., Suite 3
Eugene, OR 97401

www.wipfandstock.com

PAPERBACK ISBN: 978-1-7252-5104-5
HARDCOVER ISBN: 978-1-7252-5105-2
EBOOK ISBN: 978-1-7252-5106-9

03/16/21

To Constance

Contents

Introduction

JOHN WYCLIF HAS BEEN a polarizing figure since the middle of the fourteenth century, when he was arguing with his fellow academics at Oxford about the nature of the world and how it relates to its Creator, about the nature of God and the Church, about the sacraments (especially the Eucharist, but also penance), about the nature of authority within and without the Church, and about a host of other problems.

So problematic were Wyclif's views that he was ordered to be arrested by the pope in 1377, summoned before more than one assembly of ecclesiastics, and forced to retire from Oxford University in 1381. None of these measures was particularly effective in silencing Wyclif, who continued to publish his controversial views until his death on December 31, 1384. It was only thirty years later, at the Council of Constance, that he was formally condemned for heresy and his bones were ordered to be burned. The order was finally carried out only in 1428, when his body was exhumed, ritually stripped of the priestly office, and burned, and the ashes were scattered in a nearby river.

Wyclif's ideas, as the following pages will show, remained controversial until well into the twentieth century. Opinion about him often split along confessional lines, Protestant historians and theologians often finding him a congenial fellow traveler and Roman Catholics expounding upon the dangerous implications of his thought.

It was only in the middle of the twentieth century that these confessional interests began to fall away. Especially important for this trend was the iconoclastic work of the Oxford historian K. B. McFarlane, who sought to undo Protestant myths surrounding Wyclif in his *John Wycliffe and the Beginnings of English Nonconformity*, first published in 1952. Since that time, scholars have turned their attention to reading more closely the original works of Wyclif and contextualizing him in his place and time. There has also been a renewed interest in his philosophical works and their reception history in England and on the Continent.

The following material will look first at Wyclif's pre-Reformation reputation, including the various attempts during his own lifetime to condemn his thought, his posthumous condemnation at the Council of Constance, and the reception of his thought in England and Bohemia up to the Reformation. A second chapter will look at the characterization of Wyclif during the Reformation itself, which was a critical point for the creation of a mythos of the "Morning Star of the Reformation." Chapter 3 will explore some modern confessional constructions of Wyclif's life and times, going as far as the quincentenary of his death in

1882, and Chapter 4 will delineate the late-nineteenth-century shift from amateur to professional history and the resulting, though slow, shift in attitudes toward Wyclif that took place through to the middle of the twentieth century. A final chapter will look at work on Wyclif from the latter part of the twentieth century to today and will end with some reflections on possible avenues for the future of Wyclif studies.

1

Pre-Reformation Characterizations of Wyclif

As one historian has noted, "it is beyond the physical capacity of a lonely researcher to collect every single word of judgment passed upon Wyclyf, and there were many of them."[1] My intention here is not to provide an exhaustive study of pre-Reformation characterizations of Wyclif, but to give general outlines and impressions, to discuss what might be said about Wyclif's reputation and the use of his name in the generations after his death in 1384, and to explore the ways in which he was used for polemical purposes during the approximately one hundred years leading up to Luther's break with Rome.[2]

1. Mudroch, *Wyclyf Tradition*, xv.

2. On this topic see Mudroch, *Wyclyf Tradition*, 1–5. See also Walsh, "Wyclif's Legacy"; Bose, "Opponents of John Wyclif"; Keen, "Influence of Wyclif."

Opposition to Wyclif

Portrayals of Wyclif in the century after his death are illustrative of the various polemical uses for which he, as a theological and ecclesiastical figure, was appropriated by his opponents. The chronicler Thomas Walsingham, for instance, gives a complex picture of Wyclif, describing him as a disappointed careerist,[3] a currier of favor, an eloquent hypocrite, and a coward who became arrogant when surrounded by his powerful friends.[4] He describes Wyclif as "that old hypocrite himself, the angel of Satan and herald of Antichrist, who should not be called John Wyclif, but rather the heretic Weakbelief."[5] Walsingham makes clear his purpose for including Wyclif in his chronicle: "I have written about this in full to make it clear to everybody what great evil that monster who ascended from the abyss, that associate of Satan, John Wyclif, or Weakbelief, sowed on earth."[6] For Walsingham, Wyclif stands as an object lesson, a dangerous and seductive hypocrite who led many astray.

---

3. "eo quod iuste priuatus extiterat per archiepiscopum Cantuariensem quodam beneficio, cui iniuste incubuerat, in uniuersitate Oxoniensi situatio" (Walsingham, *St Albans Chronicle*, 74).

4. Walsingham, *St Albans Chronicle*, 76. See also 78, 80, 583–85.

5. "ipse uetus ypocrita, angelus Sathane, antichristi preambulus, non nominandus Iohannes Wyclif, uel pocius Wikkebeue, hereticu . . ." (Walsingham, *St Alban's Chronicle*, 402, translation on 403).

6. "Hec iccrico scripsi plenius ut omnibus elucescat quanta mala bestia que ascendit de abisso collega Sathane, Iohannes Wyclyff, sive Wykkebeleue, seminauit in terra" (Walsingham, *St Albans Chronicle*, 406, translation on 407).

Another of Walsingham's favorite tactics, one employed by a number of other anti-Wyclif authors, is to link Wyclif's heresies with those of past condemned heretics. In his chronicle Walsingham includes copies of a series of papal bulls sent to England in 1377 by Pope Gregory XI. These documents specifically associate Wyclif's heresies with those of Marsilius of Padua and John of Jandun, who were condemned by Pope John XXII in 1327.[7] The bull to the University of Oxford was also included in the anti-Wycliffite collection the *Fasciculi Zizaniorum* ("Bundle of Weeds"), a Carmelite production, which also sought to link Wyclif's teachings with those of past heretics, associating him especially with the condemned eucharistic theology of Berengar of Tours.[8]

These sorts of portrayals were also part of the paranoia over Lollardy apparent in the first half of the fifteenth century. The political aspects of this paranoia are treated below, but with respect to the negative portrayals of Wyclif in the polemics surrounding the early Lollard movement, there was a marked tendency to equate heresy with sedition, political dissent, and rebellion. This was apparent already in the copy of Gregory XI's bull sent to the archbishop of Canterbury and the bishop of London, in which the pope enumerates the political and social dangers inherent in the spread of heresy:

7. See Walsingham, *St Albans Chronicle*, 174–89.

8. The bull is included on 242–45 in *Fasciculi Zizaniorum*. See also 114 (where the narrative links Wyclif and Berengar), 167, 178 (where John Tyssington does the same).

> It is our will and command to your fraternity,
> that you and other masters learned in Holy Writ
> ... be zealous in informing the following people
> of these matters: Edward, the illustrious king
> of England, his beloved sons ... Joan, princess
> of Aquitaine and Wales, and other magnates in
> England, and royal counsellors; and show them
> how much damage to the devout kingdom of
> England is being done as the result of this teach-
> ing, and that not only are those very Conclusions
> erroneous in terms of the faith, but, if favourable
> notice is not taken of them they could lead to the
> destruction of the whole state.[9]

Adam of Usk, in his *Chronicon*, made a similar point about the dangers to the secular state that the teaching of Wyclif represented. He stated his fear that the undoing of the kingdom of England would come as a result of the pernicious teachings of Wyclif and his followers, who by their preaching incited

> numerous massacres, plots, disputes, quarrels
> and rebellions, which continue to this day, and
> will result, I fear, in the ruin of the kingdom ...
> The English people, turning upon each other
> because of the molten calf ... by quarrelling
> among themselves about the old faith and the

---

9. "Volumus igitur, et uestre fraternitati mandamus ... Edwardum regem Anglie illustrem, et dilectos filios ... Iohannam principissam Aquitannie et Wallie, aliosque magnates de Anglia, et consiliaros regios, per uos et alios magistros et peritos in sacra pagina ... studeatis facere plenarie informari, ac eis ostendi, quanta uerecundia deuoto regno Anglie oriatur exinde, et quod non solum sunt ipse conclusiones erronee in fide, set, si bene aduertantur, innuunt omnem destruere policiam" (Walsingham, *St Albans Chronicle*, 180, translation on 181).

new, are continually on the point of mutual de-
struction or rebellion.[10]

The people of London, Usk related, were so cor-
rupted by these heresies that it was no longer even
possible to prosecute heretics, as the great crowds
would riot and interrupt the proceedings.[11]

The Peasants' Revolt of 1381, an insurrection
during which a crowd of rebels murdered Archbishop
of Canterbury Simon Sudbury and during which the
king's uncle, John of Gaunt, was forced to flee London as his Savoy Palace was burned to the ground,[12]
likewise gave Wyclif's opponents an opportunity to
implicate his teachings in the arousal of sedition and
rebellion. Walsingham, along with his fellow chronicler Henry Knighton, and the *Fasciculi Zizaniorum*
placed the blame for the insurrection squarely at the
feet of Wyclif; Knighton and the *Fasciculi* both explicitly linked Wyclif with the famous leader of the rebels,
the priest John Ball, although it seems likely that this
was a fanciful association, as there is no actual evidence that Ball would have known Wyclif.[13]

This sort of characterization continued through-
out the fifteenth century and into the Reformation
period as well, with Roman Catholics seeking to
connect the new heretics, such as the Hussites of
Bohemia and the Reformers of the sixteenth century,

10. Usk, *The Chronicle of Adam Usk*, 7, 9.

11. Usk, *The Chronicle of Adam Usk*, 9.

12. See Hilton, *Bond Men Made Free*.

13. Walsingham, *St Albans Chronicle*, 500–503; Knighton, *Knighton's Chronicle*, 242–43; *Fasciculi Zizaniorum*, 272–73.

with the heresies of the past.[14] The council fathers at Constance, for instance, tried to yoke Jan Hus, whose teachings they also sought to condemn, with Wyclif, but they could not easily agree on what teachings of Wyclif were in fact heretical and could not successfully condemn Hus of Wycliffism, although that did not stop them from turning him over to the secular arm to be burned at the stake for heresy.[15]

Sophisticated theological opposition to Wyclif is perhaps best exemplified by English friar Thomas Netter, born around 1372, sometime confessor to both Henry V and Henry VI of England and provincial of the Carmelites in England.[16] Netter was only a teenager at most when Wyclif died, but his *Doctrinale antiquitatum fidei catholicae ecclesiae* (Doctrinal of the ancient faith of the Catholic Church) was a major anti-Wyclif work and probably the most sophisticated response to his thought. In this work, he sought to distance himself from his countryman, stating:

> Nor truly did Wyclif take anything from me, for he was not alive in my time, unless perhaps when I was a child. As God is my witness, no personal reason or any event in our time, nothing has come between us; the only reason is the attacks on the faith, deadly doctrines which lead the nation astray, deceiving and deluding innocent people, these call for some public response from us to him.[17]

14. See Kenny, "The Accursed Memory."

15. Kenny, "The Accursed Memory," 152–54; Walsh, "Wyclif's Legacy," 398.

16. See Copsey, "Thomas Netter."

17. Translation in Copsey, "Thomas Netter," 24.

The same theme of danger for the kingdom of England on account of Wyclif's deceitful teachings is present, and Netter likewise associates Wyclif with an already-condemned heresy, namely the heresy of Berenger of Tours, who had been forced to recant of errors about the Eucharist.[18] Yet Netter, who had access to several of Wyclif's works and used them extensively, more so than any other of Wyclif's opponents in the fifteenth century, made intricate theological arguments against Wyclif's teaching on such topics as extreme unction, the Eucharist, and Confirmation.[19] According to Netter, Wyclif was the inventor and supporter of what Netter called the "Lollard religion," and he was convinced that the teachings of Wyclif made disciples who went even further than their master in evil teachings. Netter therefore thought it was his duty to refute Wyclif's virulent lies.[20] Whether or not Netter was always completely fair to Wyclif—he was convinced, for instance, that Wyclif's rancor was a result of disappointment with the advancement of his ecclesiastical career, and Netter quipped that the only authority Wyclif recognized other than Scripture was his own writings—he was certainly very attentive to minute details in Wyclif's works.[21] Yet, he was scru-

18. See Levy, "Thomas Netter on the Eucharist."

19. Copsey, "Thomas Netter," 29; Hudson, "Thomas Netter's *Doctrinale* and the Lollards," 180–81. On extreme unction, see Mullins, "Netter's Defence of Extreme Unction"; on the Eucharist, see Levy, "Thomas Netter on the Eucharist"; and on confirmation, see O'Donnell, "Controversy on Confirmation."

20. Hudson, "Thomas Netter's *Doctrinale* and the Lollards," 179.

21. Hudson, "Thomas Netter's *Doctrinale* and the Lollards," 184.

pulous in his study of Wyclif so he could refute his teachings on a scriptural and patristic basis.[22]

Positive Portrayals of Wyclif

On the other side of the polemical divide, Wyclif's supporters sought to demonstrate that he was no seducer or heretic, but was rather a voice of truth crying out against abuses in Church and kingdom, and that the Church hierarchy was the true cause of the problems facing the realm.

Wyclif's support in England, despite the fears of his opponents, does seem to have faded rather quickly after his death and especially after the turn of the fifteenth century. At the very least, it had mostly been pushed underground. There is a problem of sources with respect to Lollard perceptions of Wyclif, as it seems that most of their opinions were handed on orally, and Wyclif himself is seldom mentioned explicitly in Lollard texts.[23] Nonetheless, it is possible to sketch a general picture of Lollard perceptions of him.[24] These early Lollard texts show that they perceived Wyclif as personally virtuous. William Thorpe, for instance, said that Wyclif "in his time . . . was held by many men [to be] the greatest clerk [i.e., priest] that

22. See Mullins, "Netter's Defence of Extreme Unction;" Levy, "Thomas Netter on the Eucharist"; O'Donnell, "Controversy on Confirmation."

23. Nolcken, "Another Kind of Saint," 430. There is plenty of debate about what constitutes a Lollard work. See Somerset, "Their Writings."

24. See Hornbeck, *What Is a Lollard?*

they know [of] living on Earth."[25] Other Lollards and sympathizers followed suit, with many of them, including William White; Joan Boughton, the author of *Jack Upland's Rejoinder*; and others, accounting him one of God's saints.[26] William Eamyn apparently held him to be more glorified than St. Thomas Becket, one of the most popular saints in England.[27] Interestingly enough, Eamyn is also reported to have said that "Wyclif was 'just another Catholic man who, if he were alive, would prove all his opponents heretics and Lollards,'"[28] a neat reversal of the epithet "Lollard," which could, apparently, be used as a synonym for "heretic." Lollards also drew attention to Wyclif's posthumous condemnation at the Council of Constance and the burning of his bones in 1428, arguing that he should be seen not only as a saint, but also as a martyr.[29]

In Bohemia, which had strong political and scholarly ties to England in the last years of the fourteenth century, Wyclif's reputation was quite different. There his thought was received with intellectual curiosity and even eagerness. His philosophical and theological works were studied at Charles University in Prague and were influential in the development of Jan Hus' thought, although recent scholarship has reasserted the original character of this reformer's

25. From Hudson, *Selections from English Wycliffite Writings*, 32 (my translation). On Thorpe, see Copeland, "William Thorpe and His Lollard Community," 199–221.

26. Nolcken, "Another Kind of Saint," 431–33.

27. Nolcken, "Another Kind of Saint," 433.

28. Burgess, "A Hotbed of Heresy," 56.

29. Nocklen, "Another Kind of Saint," 442–43.

ideas.[30] Hus, as was noted above, was burned at the
stake for being a Wycliffite, though it is not clear
whether that label was entirely accurate. Hus did
not accept Wyclif's interpretation of the Eucharist,
for example, which was one of the key components
of Wyclif's thought, but Hus was happy to accept
and use other of Wyclif's ideas, like the sufficiency
of the *lex Christi* (law of Christ) for governing the
Church, although even here he did not do so naively
or slavishly.[31]

The Hussite revolution was the product of
complex political and theological factors rooted in
the ideas of native thinkers, but that Wyclif's ideas
were part of the mix that made up the Czech reform
movement of the fifteenth century is beyond doubt
and demonstrates a very different reception from
that in England.

Thus it was that because of the same teachings—
as none of Wyclif's supporters denied the teachings
that his detractors accused him of—he was accounted
a damned heretic by some and a saint by others. In
fact, if it can be said that Wyclif's opponents were not
always fair to his ideas, his supporters and followers
were perhaps no better, as their understanding of
his teachings differed widely from his own writings,
even if, in the words of Patrick Hornbeck, there was

30. See Van Dussen, *From England to Bohemia*; Šmahel and Pavlicek, *A Companion to Jan Hus*. Cf. early-twentieth-century characterizations by Johann Loserth, who described Hus as a mere copycat
of Wyclif (see Loserth, *Hus und Wiclif*).

31. See Lahey, "Wyclif, the 'Hussite Philosophy,' and the Law of
Christ."

a family resemblance between their beliefs and Wyc-lif's own.[32] Thus, Wyclif was celebrated as a righteous opponent to pilgrimages and images, the idolatry of transubstantiation, and various other practices of the late-medieval Church. He was seen as an opponent of the popes, and this opposition was seen as seditious by his opponents, but as heroic and just by his follow-ers and admirers.

The Politics of Heresy

The issue of sedition highlights the need for politi-cal powers to prosecute, and persecute, heretics. As has already been noted, chroniclers such as Walsing-ham and Knighton tried to associate Wyclif with the insurrection of 1381, and purported links between Lollardy and sedition became more common in the fifteenth century and were supported by intellectu-als such as Netter.[33] Wyclif himself escaped personal condemnation in his own lifetime despite fierce op-position, and if the accounts in various chronicles are to be believed, this was due in large part to the political weight of John of Gaunt, son of Edward III and uncle to Richard II, who acted as Wyclif's protec-tor.[34] Adam of Usk thought that Wyclif was allowed to flourish because of the minority of Richard II and

32. Hornbeck, *What Is a Lollard?*

33. See Aston, "Lollardy and Sedition"; Strohm, *England's Empty Throne*.

34. See, e.g., Knighton, *Knighton's Chronicle*, 250–51; Walsing-ham, *St Albans Chronicle*, 74–75, 78–85.

the influence of Gaunt on royal policy.[35] There was, then, from these beginnings a recognition of the part that the secular arm had to play in the flourishing or suppression of heresy. This connection was well recognized by the Lancastrian kings, who had over-thrown Richard II in 1399. They were at the forefront of the development of the connection between heresy and treason, according to Paul Strohm. Henry IV, for example, immediately after his coronation, went about articulating a doctrine of "double death" in which "the condemned heretic was both burnt and hanged—or sometimes both at once—in order to suggest offense against both religious doctrine and the civil state."[36] Following the Oldcastle revolt against the Lancastrians in 1414, Sir John Oldcastle was imprisoned in the Tower of London. Upon his escape, royal proclamations that specified both the religious and political aspects of the fugitive's crimes were issued, and "the definitive linkage of heresy and treason was effected by an official proclamation (and hence statute) of Henry V's first parliament, in April 1414."[37] These developments, it might be suggested, were part of an attempt by the Lancastrian dynasty to legitimize their usurpation of the English crown in 1399. Secular influence on the reception of Wyclif did not end with the Lancastrians; even after his break with Rome, Henry VIII refused to rehabilitate Wyclif. While Wyclif's anti-papalism might have proved

35. Usk, *The Chronicle of Adam of Usk*, 3–7.
36. Strohm, *England's Empty Throne*, 133.
37. Strohm, *England's Empty Throne*, 133.

congenial to the king, his doctrine of the Eucharist was not acceptable, and as late as 1546 Wyclif's works were prohibited by royal proclamation.[38]

Conclusion

The depictions of Wyclif created by his near contemporaries, both opponents and supporters, were less concerned with an accurate portrayal of Wyclif and his thought than with a wider political or religious agenda, whether that agenda were the legitimization of the Lancastrian dynasty or the proper understanding of that most important of Christian sacraments, the Eucharist. Further, the political will of the ruling classes was vitally important to the prosecution of heresy; the Lancastrians were responsible for the suppression of Wycliffism in the fifteenth century, however successful their endeavor was in the end. Most notably, what made Wyclif a heretic to some made him a hero and a saint to others. These themes not only continued in Wyclif's reception during the Reformation, but were amplified.

38. Kenny, "The Accursed Memory," 160.

2

The Reformation and Wyclif

WYCLIF'S REPUTATION DURING THE Reformation demonstrates many of the themes that have been developed in the first chapter, with both sides of the debate vaunting or condemning Wyclif for one and the same opinion. Over time, however, Wyclif's opinions had become less well known. If at the Council of Constance the list of condemned articles was something of a caricature of Wyclif's thought, by the time of Luther's break with Rome, the caricature had drifted into the territory of myth. This reality would not change much until the nineteenth century, and even then only very slowly. In particular, it was the mythology of the "Morning Star of the Reformation" that would dominate theological and historical understandings of Wyclif for more than three hundred years.

Reformer as Warmed-Over Medieval Heretic

Famously, John Eck, Martin Luther's opponent in a disputation at Leipzig in July 1519, pointed out to

Luther that he was teaching the heresies of Wyclif and Hus, saying further:

> I surmise that it must be horrible for all Christian believers that the reverend Father [i.e., Luther] does not hesitate to speak against the sacred and honourable Council of Constance, gathered with the great consent of Christendom, by asserting that some of the articles of Wiclif and Huss were most Christian and evangelical . . . which the universal Church could not condemn.[1]

It seems clear that the tactic was to group Luther together with already-condemned heresies and to add the weight of the decisions of a recognized authority, in this case the Council of Constance, to Eck's own arguments against Luther and his reformist ideas. This was not a new tactic, as the idea of connecting new heresies with those of the past was already used against both Wyclif and Hus. The tactic was taken up again in the papal bull *Exsurge Domine*, which excommunicated Luther:

> Reputable men have reported to us what we can hardly express without fearfulness and pain. We have unfortunately seen and read with our own eyes many and various errors, some of which have already been condemned by the councils and definitions of our predecessors, since they incorporate the heresies of the Greeks and Bohemians.[2]

---

1. From *The Reformation in Its Own Words*, edited by Hans J. Hillerbrand, 69–70.

2. "Exsurge Domine," in Hillerbrand, *The Reformation in Its Own Words*, 81.

These errors were all the more abhorrent to the pope, since the Germans had historically been friends of the Roman Church, helping to condemn the heresies of the "Hussites, of Wiclif and Jerome of Prague at the Council of Constance."[3] Henry VIII of England had likewise made the connection between Luther and Wyclif and connected their thought with sedition and rebellion.[4]

The Council of Trent likewise made the connection, as did such Roman Catholic polemicists as Thomas Harding, Nicholas Harpsfield, and Robert Parsons.[5] These three men, in their polemics against Protestant historians such as John Bale, John Foxe, and John Jewel, were at pains to demonstrate that Wyclif was not only a heretic, but also an "uncomfortable ally for the reformers: Wyclif approved of the worship of relics and images," as Harpsfield claimed in a less than nuanced statement.[6] Parsons noted that Wyclif could not be truly called a martyr, for he had not actually died for his beliefs nor been exiled or even imprisoned. In Parsons' opinion Wyclif, who was called by the Reformers "holy Elias, and brother-like Saint Wyclif," was really "one of the most pernicious, wicked, dissembling, hypocritical impugners of Christ and his doctrine, that ever was in the Church of God . . . And this . . . is the

3. "Exsurge Domine," 81.

4. Kenny, "The Accursed Memory," 159; Aston, "John Wycliffe's Reformation Reputation," 31.

5. Kenny, "The Accursed Memory," 161–66.

6. Kenny, "The Accursed Memory," 163.

protestant's great grandfather, so much bragged of by Fox and Bale."[7] He also argued that Wyclif's theology was Donatist, that is, that Wyclif held that a bishop or priest in mortal sin could not exercise his office or perform the sacraments.[8] Clearly, the point was to demonstrate to the Reformers that their hero was not who they thought he was and that Wyclif held positions on important Reformation questions that were, in fact, the opposite of the Reformed position.

Medieval Heretics as Precursors to the Reformers

Despite the efforts to make Wyclif out to be a poor reformer, he remained for the Reformers of the sixteenth century a hero and a precursor of their own efforts.[9] William Tyndale, who shall be discussed further below, in a reversal of the opinion that Wyclif's teachings were the cause of sedition and rebellion, made the argument that it was a failure to heed Wyclif's warning and call to repentance that was the cause of disaster. Wyclif, Tyndale said in his "Prologue to Jonah" (1531),

> preached repentance unto our fathers not long
> since. They repented not; for their hearts were
> indurate, and their eyes blinded with their own
> pope-holy righteousness, wherewith they had

7. Quoted in Aston, "John Wycliffe's Reformation Reputation," 39, spelling and punctuation modernized.

8. Kenny, "The Accursed Memory," 165.

9. See Aston, "John Wycliffe's Reformation Reputation," 23–51.

made their souls gay against the receiving again
of the wicked spirit.[10]

The failure to heed Wyclif's call to repentance
resulted in the murder of King Richard II and the
Wars of the Roses in the fifteenth century and
brought England, in the opinion of Tyndale, "half
into a wilderness."[11]

It was John Bale who took the decisive step in
creating the mythos of Wyclif the proto-Protestant,
for it was he who dubbed Wyclif *stella matutina*, "the
Morning Star"; he went beyond the Lollard characterization of Wyclif, writing of him:

> John Wycliffe, Englishman, the greatest theo-
> logian of his time, held alone for many years
> the magisterial chair (as it is called) in teaching
> and disputing at Oxford. Apart from the truly
> apostolic life which he led, he far excelled all
> his fellows in England by his ability, eloquence,
> and erudition.[12]

Whereas Netter had been ashamed of his fellow
countryman and sought to distance himself from
Wyclif and his movement, Bale proudly and promi-
nently announced Wyclif's Englishness and vaunted
his intellectual prowess. Bale saw himself as Wyclif's successor in the fight for evangelical truth and
emphasized the role of the English in the quest for
reform. As one historian has noted,

10. Aston, "John Wycliffe's Reformation Reputation," 24.

11. Aston, "John Wycliffe's Reformation Reputation," 24.

12. Bale, *Illustrium maioris Britanniae scriptorum* [. . .] *sum-marium*, quoted in translation in Aston, "John Wycliffe's Reformation Reputation," 25.

in Bale's history, John Wyclif emerges as the central English author. Aside from the dedicatory
portrait of Bale himself, the woodcut of Wyclif is
the only image of a British author in [the *Illustrium maioris Britanniae scriptorum*] *Summarium*.
Both Wyclif and Bale are seen in the evangelical
pose with book in hand.[13]

John Foxe's work and conception of history followed on from Bale, taking up his division of history into five three-hundred-year-long eras. The first
three hundred years were the age of the purity of the
Church, and the next three hundred years, beginning with the advent of Constantine, were a period
of quiet. The period following that, marked by the
assumption of the papal title and the rise of Islam,
was the beginning of the decline of the Church. The
decline accelerated in the fourth period with the nec-
romancy of Pope Sylvester I and the greed of Pope
Gregory VII. Finally, the fifth period began with the
advent of Wyclif and the loosing of Satan in the form
of opposition to Wyclif and his followers.[14] Wyclif
marked the beginning of the end of the world, the last
age, when true Christians would be persecuted, but
reform would finally overcome the Church's decay.

Both Bale and Foxe established Wyclif and the
Lollards as precursors to the Reformation and made
a strong connection between them and other heretics
of the past, just as Roman Catholic authors did, but
they did it for the opposite purpose. These heretics

13. King, *English Reformation Literature*, 70.

14. Levy, "The Reformation and English History Writing,"
99–100.

took on a very different meaning for the Reformers, who saw them as champions of truth fighting against the corruptions and errors of Rome. Thus, Bale celebrated Berengar of Tours for his attack on the Roman doctrine of the Mass, Marsilius of Padua for his attack on the hierarchy, and Wyclif, Hus, Luther, and other reformers as "a tradition of learned opposition."[15] There was also something of a nationalistic tone in Foxe, who asserted that England had kept its purity longer than other realms and was, through Wyclif, the first to re-establish this purity.[16] Another Reformer, John Aylmer, also sounded this nationalistic note: "Our countryman and brother John Wyclif begat Hus, who begat Luther, who begat truth."[17] The pride of the English Reformers in their countryman, and their rehabilitation of medieval heretics, contrasts sharply with the attitude of their opponents; once again the two sides of the debate agreed on a series of facts, but drew opposite conclusions as to their meaning and significance.

The continued importance of political will and the secular arm for the prosecution of heresy is demonstrated neatly in the way in which the University of Oxford dealt with the arrival of Lutheran writings in England. In the early 1520s, the University and its scholars became involved in the king's plans to refute the writings of Luther and his "new Wycliffism." The

15. Levy, "The Reformation and English History Writing," 90.

16. Levy, "The Reformation and English History Writing," 101, 123.

17. Aylmer, *An Harborowe*, quoted in Collinson, "Thomas Cranmer," 81–82.

strongest work to come out of the university was authored by Edward Powell, who took Wyclif to be "a *symbol*, as well as the fount of all of Luther's important deviations."[18] These efforts were part of a larger attempt by the University to distance itself, under pressure from the English Crown, from the heresy of Wyclif, a once-respected scholar who spent the vast majority of his career at the university.[19] By the end of the century, however, the University was emphasizing its Protestant heritage, attempting to distance itself from a Jesuit alumnus who had recently been burned.[20] One can sense that there was something of a once-bitten, twice-shy motivation at work at Oxford. Since they had been caught out and embarrassed by Wyclif, they were reluctant to press their luck with the new doctrines emerging on the Continent, especially against the royal will. Once that will had changed, however, they were ready enough to follow suit. This was another example of how rulers could rather drastically affect the religious situation within their territories as well as the voiced opinions about particular religious figures.

Wyclif's place in the dispute between William Tyndale and Thomas More over the translation of the Scriptures into the vernacular is a clear demonstration of the relativity of the heterodox/orthodox dichotomy. Both Tyndale and More accepted that Wyclif had

18. Lytle, "John Wyclif, Martin Luther and Edward Powell," 474.

19. Lytle, "John Wyclif, Martin Luther and Edward Powell," 465–66.

20. Lytle, "John Wyclif, Martin Luther and Edward Powell," 478–79.

translated the whole of Scripture into English, but this supposed fact held very different meaning for each of them. More, in the same way that he treated Tyndale's translation, argued that Wyclif had intentionally mistranslated the Scriptures in order to make it appear as if they supported Wyclif's heresies.[21] Tyndale, on the other hand, thought it no heresy to translate the Scriptures into the vernacular, and he pointed to the many existing translations. In fact, as will be seen in the discussion of later Protestant treatments of Wyclif, it became axiomatic that he had translated the Bible into English, and this supposed accomplishment was one of the most important acts of Wyclif's career for his Protestant promoters, who saw him as a champion of the Bible who placed it in the hands of the common people in defiance to the ecclesiastical hierarchy's desire to conserve Scripture's truth for themselves alone.[22] Whether or not Wyclif was responsible for the Middle English translation of the Bible—and the modern consensus is that he was not—did not really matter; everyone thought that he had translated the Bible, and they either condemned him for it, finding his translation aberrant and heretical, or praised him for returning the gospel to the people from whom it had been hidden for far too long.[23]

The testimony of William Eamyn, which was noted in the previous chapter, is also demonstrative of the point that heresy was a relative term:

21. More, *A Dialogue Concerning Heresies*, 314–17.

22. Aston, "John Wycliffe's Reformation Reputation," 30.

23. See below, chapters 4 and 5.

"Wyclif was 'just another Catholic man who, if he were alive, would prove all his opponents heretics and Lollards.'"[24] The meaning of the terms seem to have been malleable, changing to suit the needs of the author. It was common, in fact, for Reformers to turn the term "heretic" back on their accusers, much as it was common for medieval heretics, like Wyclif himself, to do likewise.[25] "If, in fundamental issues of medieval society, heresy is just the other side of the coin," writes Alexander Patchovsky:

> then we can expect that the use of the term *heretic* . . . is not reserved to the triumphant Church militant, but is also common to its less successful opponents . . . We might look at . . . Wyclif with his Hussite adherents, and how—as they saw it—not only a single pope as a person, but the whole papacy as an institution became not only heretical, but downright 'antichrist.'[26]

This was one of the reasons why the Reformers celebrated medieval heretics; they were certain that they had found kindred spirits who were only called heretics because they had dared to stand up to the papacy, which was the true source of evil in the Church.

Conclusion

Wyclif's reputation among Reformers firmly established the mythos about him. He was, from then on,

24. Burgess, "A Hotbed of Heresy," 56.

25. See Friesen, "Medieval Heretics or Forerunners of the Reformation," 165–89; esp. Patchovsky, "Heresy and Society," 23–41.

26. Patchovsky, "Heresy and Society," 40–41.

the persecuted champion of the gospel who sought only to give the gospel back to the people and destroy the idolatry and heresy that had infected the Church for going on several centuries. This was an incredibly durable portrait of the man, as the following chapters will show.

3

Wyclif in Modern
Confessional Histories

DURING THE SEVENTEENTH AND eighteenth
centuries, little changed in the way of portrayals of
Wyclif, apart from a biography of note by John Lewis,
*The History of the Life and Sufferings of the Reverend
and Learned John Wiclif, D.D.*, published in 1720.
Lewis was himself learned, and he looked to earlier
sources, such as the chronicles of Walsingham and
Usk, and included many of them in his book. He also
included a list of Latin and English writings attributed to Wyclif , believing, in contrast to more recent
historiography, that all of these works were authen-
tic.[1] Learned as he was, however, Lewis was clearly
partisan, referring at times to "popish" doctrines, and
as the book's title indicates, his portrayal was meant
to highlight Wyclif's righteous suffering against the
abuses and corruptions of the Church.

---

1. Lewis, *History of the Life and Sufferings*, 143–74. None of the
English works once attributed to Wyclif are considered authentically
wycliffian by contemporary scholars.

In the nineteenth century there were again major advances. That century saw the publication of several of Wyclif's Latin works, sparked by the interest of confessional historians and especially by the approaching quincentenary of his death, an event that was marked in 1884 and that saw an explosion of biographies, mostly derivative, as well as the foundation of the Wyclif Society by F. J. Furnivall, which was responsible for the publication of the majority of Wyclif's works.

One of the first major biographies of the nineteenth century was that by congregationalist minister Robert Vaughan, *The Life and Opinions of John Wycliffe, D.D.*, published in two volumes in 1828 and again in 1831. He also published *Tracts and Treatises of John de Wycliffe*, a selection of translations from Wyclif's Latin works along with English tracts thought to have been penned by Wyclif, in 1845. A second book on Wyclif, *John de Wycliffe, DD: A Monograph*, was published in 1853. The opening words of Vaughan's 1831 biography of Wyclif set the tone for the rest of his work on the reformer:

> The name of John de Wycliffe appears in the page of history, as that of the first Englishman whose views of Christianity were such as to induce a renunciation of the spiritual as well as the temporal power claimed by the pontiffs; and to his mind, nearly every principle of our general Protestantism may be distinctly traced. To diffuse his doctrine among his countrymen, was the object to which his energies were directed in the face of every danger, with an industry which is almost incredible, and with a success which

his enemies describe as a leading cause of the
revolution which signalized the reign of Henry
the eighth.[2]

Once again Wyclif was depicted as the proto-
Reformer, the Morning Star, facing down all danger
in order to spread the (Protestant) gospel. The myth
of Wyclif had remained strong, and a direct line had
been drawn from Wyclif to Protestantism. Vaughan,
like Lewis before him, was very learned, and in
fact he personally used the manuscripts containing
Wyclif's works, traveling to Oxford and Cambridge,
Dublin, and London to study the works of the "Father of the Reformation."[3]

Vaughan's work was important in part because of
the number of imitators he inspired; the great boom
of biographies that appeared at the end of the century was full of works drawing heavily on Vaughan's
scholarship. None of these later books rose to a very
distinguished level of scholarship, certainly none
equal to the work of Vaughan himself. Rather, they
repeated the Protestant myths already developed by
other authors.[4]

Editorial work began in earnest with the contributions of Gotthard Lechler, who published an edition
of *De officio pastorali* in 1863 and of *Trialogus* in 1869.
Lechler also wrote a biography of Wyclif published in

2. Lewis, *History of the Life and Sufferings*, iii.

3. Lewis, *History of the Life and Sufferings*, v–vi.

4. By my count there are at least seventeen of these biographies
in English. None of these works are listed in the bibliography, but
they are available for download from the Lollard Society website:
https://lollardsociety.org/?page_id=10.

1873, *Johannes von Wiclif und die Vorgeschichte der Reformation*. This work was translated into English as *John Wycliffe and His English Precursors* and first appeared in 1878, to be revised and reprinted several times into the early twentieth century. Lechler was a Lutheran pastor and theologian who trained at Tübingen under Ferdinand Christian Baur, although he did not attach himself to the Tübingen school subsequently. His interest in Wyclif was quite clearly confessional; as the original, German title of his biography suggests, he was interested in demonstrating how Wyclif, always for Lechler the Morning Star, held Reformed theological positions prior to the Reformation.[5]

The approach of the quincentenary of Wyclif's death proved irresistible for a number of Protestant scholars and churchmen. As has been noted, F. J. Furnivall founded the Wyclif Society in 1882, and myriad derivative (Protestant) biographies of Wyclif proliferated. Wycliffe Hall was founded at Oxford in 1877, and the Protestant Episcopal Divinity School, founded in Toronto in 1877, changed its name to Wycliffe College unofficially between 1882 and 1883 and then officially, by a court ruling, in 1885.[6]

All of these efforts were enmeshed with strong religious conviction, specifically a sort of boosterism for Protestantism, mixed with an often tacit, but just as often explicit, British nationalism. All of the editors for the Wyclif Society were strongly Protestant, often of evangelical persuasion, with the one exception

5. See Lahey, introduction to *Trialogus*, 30–31.
6. See Otto, "Word of God."

being a Roman Catholic who conducted his work despite his disagreement with Wyclif's doctrine. That editor, Michael Dziewicki, felt the need to explain his work with the Wyclif Society:

> People have asked me many a time how I, nominally a Catholic, could aid in publishing the works of one so contrary to Catholicism as Wyclif is universally considered to be; and they readily supposed that I was indeed a Catholic only in name. They mistook; and though I have sincerely—and I hope successfully—tried to edit Wyclif with perfect impartiality from first to last, I have no sympathy with those of his doctrines that contradict the teaching of my Church. When I was offered the position of editor of Wyclif's Latin works, I consulted a clergyman of my faith in London. He told me that a translation into the vernacular would be forbidden, but that a mere edition of the Latin text was quite another thing. I have since had reason to doubt whether his ruling was technically right; but there is no doubt whatever that it was right practically, and that I at any rate, as a layman asking counsel, was right in accepting it. 'Qui s'excuse, s'accuse', but this is rather a justification than an excuse.[7]

Dziewicki's words speak volumes. Placed in a position—tempted, one might say—to undertake work on the project, he eased his conscience by consulting a "clergyman of my faith" (a turn of phrase that creates separation from the Protestant editors of the Wyclif Society) because he knew well that he would be working on material containing "doctrines that contradict the teaching of [his] Church." The status

---

7. Dziewicki, Preface to *De ente librorum duorum*, vi.

of Latin as a sort of code language was used as a reason that a Roman Catholic might edit Wyclif's Latin works; the language was used to hide Wyclif's errors and questionable doctrines. This strategic leveraging of Latin's inaccessibility stands in stark contrast to the Protestant celebration of English translations of the Bible as a means of making Scripture accessible. Yet despite his doubts about the validity of the priest's advice, Dziewicki as a layman was able to justify his work on the project by recourse to a strong clerical/lay distinction quite foreign to the Protestantism of his fellow editors.

Furnivall and the Wyclif Society in general sought to rescue Wyclif from the dishonor of having his principal works left to rot away in manuscript. They saw Wyclif as a paragon of Reformed theology and a champion of the English language and people, and it was hugely important that he was thought to have translated the Bible into Middle English. On these grounds Furnivall courted the evangelical wing of the Church of England.[8]

Because of some curious twists and turns of history, the manuscripts of Wyclif's works survived in about equal numbers in England, Prague, and Vienna, a reality that presented numerous logistical problems for the Society.[9] Several Continental scholars, all but one of them German-speaking, acted as the main editors for the society, and the complex political and religious situation of nineteenth-century

8. Spencer, "F. J. Furnivall's Last Fling," 791, 799–800.

9. See Hudson, *Studies in the Transmission of Wyclif's Writings*.

Europe played into their estimation of Wyclif. They were raising, in the words of Rudolph Buddensieg, one of the Society's editors, a monument "more beautiful and durable than marble or bronze, not formed of lifeless stone, but moulded in his own living words of evangelical faith, of manly frankness, and patriotic high-mindedness."[10]

Montagu Burrows was an active member of the English Church Union (an Anglo-Catholic organization), acting as the chairman of the Oxford branch for a time, and of the Universities' Mission to Central Africa, serving as secretary to the Oxford branch. He was also the first Chichele professor of modern history at Oxford University.[11] Burrows delivered a series of lectures that became a biography of Wyclif, first published in 1881, that, it has been suggested, might have inspired the naming of Wycliffe College in Toronto.[12] Here is how he characterized Wyclif:

> [Wyclif was] surnamed by his contemporaries 'the Evangelical Doctor.' The title was prophetic. Long before he became the reformer of England and Europe, he attained his extraordinary eminence in the Schools by, or at least in connection with, his intimate knowledge of what was then almost a sealed book, the Bible. To what sources he owed the impulse given to his Bible studies is a question involved in too much obscurity to justify treatment in these Lectures. Peter Waldo's

10. Buddensieg, *Polemical Works*, 1:xi, quoted in Spencer, "F. J. Furnivall's Last Fling," 8.

11. *Oxford Dictionary of National Biography*, s.v. "Montagu Burrows, 1819–1905."

12. See Otto, "Word of God," 305.

followers were Biblemen, not heretics; and the
University system was a ready means of inter-
communication. Possibly it may have come
through that channel.[13]

This is an extraordinary portrait; the only ele-
ment based in reality is Wyclif's cognomen *doctor
evangelicus*, which some of his followers, both in
England and on the Continent, did in fact call him.
Burrows' portrait is in essence a Protestant stereotype of Wyclif and of the Middle Ages, and it was
this sort of stereotype that so drew the admiration
of the evangelical wing of the Anglican Church in
England, in Ireland, and in Canada. These men were
very concerned about the rise of ritualism and Anglo-
Catholicism, and they placed especial emphasis on
the role of the Bible in theology, in Church history,
and in the ongoing practice of the Church. Wyclif's
name became popular with them as a symbol of their
own theology, especially since he was supposed to
have translated the Bible out of Latin into English,
out of a language "not understood of the people," as
Article XXIV of the *Thirty-Nine Articles of Religion*
has it.[14] The principles here are clearly confessional
and driven, in large part, by ecclesiastical politics.

The foundation of Wycliffe College in Toronto is
an interesting case study of the popular reception of
the Wyclif Myth. Founded as the Protestant Episcopal Divinity School in 1877 and born of the partisan
strife within the Diocese of Toronto in the nineteenth

13. Burrows, *Wiclif's Place in History*, 48.

14. *Articles of Religion*, 707.

century, the College was founded on sound evangelical principles. The name of the school was changed, first unofficially and then officially, to Wycliffe College, the choice being based on the portrayal of Wyclif as a proto-Reformer, the Morning Star, whose name alone stood for the evangelical Protestant theology of the founders. These founders were not men of little consequence. They had connections both with the University of Toronto—Daniel Wilson was a trustee of the University—and with the provincial government and wider Canadian society; the influential Blake family had strong connections with the founding of Wycliffe, for instance. One of the early influential members of the Wycliffe faculty, George M. Wrong, is worth discussing in some detail in the next chapter, as his career marks a transition from confessional to professional historiographical method in relation to the study of Wyclif.[15]

The Protestant myth of Wyclif continued to dominate portrayals of the man until the end of the nineteenth century. Even the grand editorial work of the Wyclif Society, to which subsequent scholarship owes an enormous debt, was motivated by this persistent mythos. The entrenched view of Wyclif as a reformer before the Reformers did not go away quietly, in part, no doubt, because he was useful as a myth and symbol for Protestants such as the founders of Wycliffe College, who could make him stand in for evangelical Protestant theology.

15. For this paragraph, see Otto, "Word of God."

4

Wyclif in the Hands of Professional Historians

As NOTED IN THE previous chapter, there was a flurry of activity around the quincentenary of Wyclif's death, leading to a number of confessional, derivative biographies; the foundation of a pair of colleges; and the editorial project of the Wyclif Society, all founded to one extent or another on the Protestant myth of Wyclif as the Morning Star of the Reformation. As the nineteenth century waned, the writing of history became more and more professional, and while confessional interests continued to be an important motivator in Wyclif studies, the first half of the twentieth century was a period of transition away from amateur, confessional biographies and studies and toward professional, more detached investigations.

From Confessional to Professional

Two historians, one Canadian and the other English, can be taken as representative of the

late-nineteenth- and early-twentieth-century portrayals of Wyclif. The first, George M. Wrong, was
instrumental in the professionalization of history in
Canada. The second, Herbert Workman, wrote what
is still the most comprehensive biography of Wyclif.
While their work still shows a demonstrable confessional bent, the two men were concerned with developing more thoroughgoing methodologies than those
of their predecessors, and their work may be seen as
constituting a shift from the heroic, myth-making
portrayals of Wyclif to a more objective portrayal.

George M. Wrong, born in 1860 in southwest-
ern Ontario, was educated at University College and
Wycliffe College, entering both in 1879 and graduat-
ing in 1883. He was ordained in the Anglican Church,
but instead of taking a parish, he taught Church history and apologetics at Wycliffe through to 1892,
while also taking time to study abroad in Berlin and
at Oxford. Following the death of Daniel Wilson in
1892, Wrong took up a lectureship at the University
of Toronto and in 1894 was appointed professor of
history and ethnology.[1]

Wrong emphasized in his inaugural address a
kind of golden mean for historical studies. On the one
hand, it was not to be presumed that simply anyone
could be an expert in history, though almost anyone
with an education knew something of the subject.
"Men who have not given an hour's serious study to
historical questions will assume the tone of experts
and critics with a lightheartedness that is amazing,"

1. Wright, *Professionalization*, 29–31.

he wrote.[2] On the other hand, historians, although they were to be experts and to base their arguments on primary sources, manuscript as well as print, were not to make history mysterious and inaccessible to the amateur.[3] Wrong's career in Toronto represents important shifts in late-nineteenth-century historiography; in 1896 he founded the *Review of Historical Publications Relating to Canada* (later *The Canadian Historical Review*) under the influence of "the German seminar, the American Historical Association, the *English Historical Review*, and the *American Historical Review*."[4] This publication served to delimit the historical profession as well as to emphasize the scientific study of history and its basis in primary-documentary evidence.[5]

Yet for all his work at professionalizing history, Wrong's characterization of Wyclif was not free of confessional interests, a fact that is of little surprise for a late-nineteenth-century Anglican clergyman, although he did, to his credit, actually read Wyclif's works. In his 1892 study of the English crusade to Flanders in 1383, Wrong demonstrates clear sympathy with Wyclif's attacks on the friars and monks and seems to have swallowed whole the anti-fraternal satires of the Late Middle Ages.[6] It is a little odd that Wyclif should be given such prominence in Wrong's

2. Wrong, *Historical Study in the University*, non-paginated, quoted in Wright, *Professionalization of History*, 31.

3. Wright, *Professionalization*, 31.

4. Wright, *Professionalization*, 32.

5. Wright, *Professionalization*, 32–33.

6. See, e.g., Wrong, *Crusade of 1383*, 32–33.

study—he is mentioned more than a dozen times and given center stage for a whole section of one chapter—for Wyclif had little to do with the crusade apart from denouncing it, and in this he was very much in the minority of opinion; the crusade seems to have been very popular before the campaign itself, which was disastrous and led to the crusade's leader, Bishop Henry Despenser of Norwich, being impeached by Parliament and turning popular opinion against it.[7] Wrong's preference seems less odd upon consideration of his description of Wyclif as "the most striking figure in England at this period."[8] This is an estimation that would seem exaggerated to most, if not all, modern scholars of Wyclif, and in the end, Wrong leaves another portrait of the proto-Reformer who takes all of his significance from opposition to the excesses and errors of the medieval English Church.

Nonetheless, Wrong marks a decided turn in the study of Wyclif, although it would take a few generations truly to take hold. Wyclif was still, for the first half of the twentieth century, of interest mostly to Protestants. Cardinal Gasquet was about the only Roman Catholic voice of any significance with regard to Wyclif in this period, and his opinion was that Wyclif did not translate the Bible into English, attacking one of the foundations of the Protestant myth.[9] Dyson

7. See Wilks, "Roman Candle."

8. Wrong, *Crusade of 1383*, 46.

9. Gasquet, "The Pre-Reformation English Bible"; Gasquet, *The Old English Bible*. Gasquet's position that the Wycliffite Bible was a Catholic translation has recently been defended by H. A. Kelly (*The Middle English Bible*, see esp. 141–46).

Hague, a member of the faculty at Wycliffe College as well as an alumnus, wrote a biography of Wyclif in 1909 that was subsequently republished in an expanded edition in 1935. This was a work that had clearly confessional purposes and was indeed meant, at least implicitly, for supporters of the College, characterizing Wyclif as a good evangelical and a "glorious name to live up to."[10]

A much more important and influential work was the two-volume biography of Wyclif by the Methodist minister and historian Herbert Workman, published in 1926. Workman was a circuit minister in England in the late nineteenth century before becoming principal at Westminster Teacher Training College at Oxford. He lectured at Vanderbilt University in 1916 and at the University of Chicago in 1927.[11]

Workman's biography of Wyclif was somewhat romantic and bought into the Reformation myths of the proto-Reformer. For example, it was fundamental to Workman that Wyclif translated the Scriptures into English and composed English tracts for the use of his order of Poor Preachers. The portrait was an idealized one that was easily imagined by a Methodist circuit minister. The Poor Preacher, or Poor Priest,

> in the highways and byways and by the village greens and graveyards, sometimes even in the churches, should denounce abuse, proclaim the true doctrine of the Eucharist, and teach the

---

10. Hague, *Life and Work of John Wycliffe*, 199.

11. See Harmon, *The Encyclopedia of World Methodism*, 2599.

right thinking from which, as [Wyclif] deemed,
right living would follow.[12]

In this portrait Wyclif was depicted as the central
cog in a mission of re-evangelization in England, a
fourteenth-century John Wesley.[13] Yet Workman was
not uncritical in his evaluation of Wyclif and his Poor
Preachers. He noted that the Preachers would have
been ordained clergymen, not laymen like some later
Lollard preachers, thus calling into question Wyclif's
Preachers as precursors to Luther's doctrine of the
priesthood of all believers.[14] Nonetheless, Workman's
portrayal of Wyclif sending out the Poor Priests was
somewhat fanciful:

> Clad in russet robes of undressed wool reaching
> to their feet (a garb which Wyclif had assumed
> at Canterbury [Hall at Oxford]), without san-
> dals, purse, or scrip, a long staff in their hand,
> dependent for food and shelter on the goodwill
> of their neighbours, their only possession a few
> pages of Wyclif's Bible (especially the transla-
> tion of the gospels and epistles for the day), his
> tracts and sermons, moving constantly from
> place to place like the early Methodist preachers
> in their "circuits"—for Wyclif feared as Wesley
> also feared lest they should become 'possession-
> ers', tied to one place like a dog,—given not 'to
> frequenting taverns, hunting, or to chess', but
> 'to duties which befit the priesthood, studious
> acquaintance with God's law, plain preaching
> of the word of God, and devout thankfulness',

12. Workman, *John Wyclif*, 2:201.
13. Workman, *John Wyclif*, 2:201.
14. Workman, *John Wyclif*, 2:202.

Wyclif's 'poor priest', like the friars before them, soon became a power in the land.[15]

This portrait cannot exactly be called objective. Certain scholars in the twentieth century would go so far as to dismiss entirely the idea of Wyclif sending out Poor Preachers, arguing that such Preachers never, in fact, existed.[16] One need not go that far in order to object to an exaggerated and romanticized depiction of Wyclif as a precursor to Methodism.

For all that, Workman was a serious and thorough scholar. A good example of his seriousness and thoroughness is his take on the myth that Wyclif was at one point a member of Parliament. The idea was argued by Gotthard Lechler, who thought that Wyclif's reference to himself as "peculiaris regis clericus" (in a special way the king's cleric)[17] might be interpreted to mean that Wyclif had been member of Parliament.[18] Workman rejected this idea outright as completely without historical merit, pointing to the fact that clergy were not eligible to assume such a role: "That Wyclif may have had a place in Convocation[19] as one of the representatives of the inferior clergy, or as the proctor for some official, is possible, but that he could ever have been summoned, except indeed purely

---

15. Workman, *John* Wyclif, 2:203–4.

16. See the next section below.

17. Wyclif, *Opera minora*, 422.

18. Lechler, *John Wycliffe and His English Precursors*,130–33.

19. Convocation is the meeting of the bishops and clergy of the Province of Canterbury or York. During the Middle Ages, it often met in conjunction with Parliament. It was prorogued by the British Crown between 1717 and 1852.

formally under the *praemunientes* clause,[20] as such a representative to the Commons is almost inconceivable, and certainly without historical justification."[21] Workman points rather to the uncontested evidence that Wyclif worked for the English government—for example, in a diplomatic mission to Bruges to discuss papal taxation—in order to explain Wyclif's phrase, a more sound historical judgment.[22]

Despite its faults from the viewpoint of modern, non-confessional, professional history, Workman's biography remains a standard reference work in Wyclif studies on account of its thoroughness, seriousness, and detail. Workman's has yet to be surpassed in terms of a biography of Wyclif, and it might be some time yet until it is, as most contemporary studies are quite specialized, as will be seen in the next chapter.

Professional Historians and the Myth of John Wyclif

The intermediate phase of Wyclif studies represented by Wrong and Workman, one in which confessional interests mixed with the emerging trends of the professionalization of history, ended with the publication of K. B. McFarlane's 1952 *John Wycliffe and the Beginnings of English Non-Conformity*, which sought impartiality in its treatment of Wyclif in order to

20. This clause ordered bishops to bring certain members of their cathedral and diocese with them to Parliament in an attempt by the Crown to control the Church.

21. Workman, *John Wyclif*, 1:237.

22. Workman, *John Wyclif*, 1:239.

remove what McFarlane called "several layers of rich brown protestant varnish."[23] McFarlane, most widely known for his studies of late-medieval aristocracy and "bastard feudalism,"[24] himself held no religious beliefs and approached Wyclif from a position of something like objectivity, and he certainly did not have a confessional interest in his assessment of Wyclif. McFarlane's aim was, in fact, iconoclastic;[25] he sought, by removing those layers of varnish, to undo the mythmaking of Bale and Foxe. His resulting biography was none too flattering for the reformer-priest. He referred to Wyclif's "catastrophic incompetence as a practical reformer,"[26] called Wyclif's predestinarianism (a more subtle doctrine than McFarlane gave credit for) a "grisly creed,"[27] and characterized the man as a bitterly disappointed careerist, echoing the attacks of Wyclif's monastic opponents.[28]

While McFarlane recognized that Wyclif had an immense impact on England through Lollardy, a movement that McFarlane found surprisingly resilient, he had very little time for the Poor Priests so beloved of Workman:

23. McFarlane, *Wycliffe*, 10.

24. *Oxford Dictionary of National Biography*, s.v. "McFarlane, (Kenneth) Bruce."

25. McFarlane acknowledged as much: "The first task of an impartial biographer must therefore be destructive: to free his subject from a great deal of ignorant repainting and several layers of rich brown protestant varnish" (McFarlane, *John Wycliffe*, 10).

26. McFarlane, *John Wycliffe*, 186.

27. McFarlane, *John Wycliffe*, 92.

28. McFarlane, *John Wycliffe*, 63–68. See also the section in Chapter 1 of the present book entitled "Opposition to Wyclif."

> In any case it is hard to believe that by 1377 Wycliffe was ready to take the decisive step of sending his apostles, clad in russet gowns and barefoot like pilgrims, on missionary journeys round England. The view that he did not do it then but never did it is, to say the least, a tenable one; since by 1382, when there is indisputable evidence of unlicensed Lollard preaching, he was no longer at Oxford, and there is nothing then or later to connect his refuge at Lutterworth to the movement. The dispatch of missionaries on tour may well have been the work of younger hotheads.[29]

One senses that there might be an underlying animosity in this use of an argument from silence, since it is remarkable that McFarlane should accept the witness of chroniclers in his characterization of Wyclif as a disappointed careerist, but would reject that same witness when it comes to Wyclif dispatching preachers. McFarlane would not accept other arguments either:

> Against this must be set the fervent belief of modern writers that Wycliffe's books from 1377 onwards contain frequent references under various names to his 'Poor Priests'. But an examination of the cited passages lends no support whatever to the hypothesis; the possessive pronoun and the capital letters had no contemporary warrant and to call the Wycliffites 'Poor Priests' is to be guilty of a nineteenth-century anachronism.[30]

---

29. McFarlane, *John Wycliffe*, 101.
30. McFarlane, *John Wycliffe*, 101.

Unfortunately, since the book began as a series of lectures and was published with limited scholarly apparatus, McFarlane's analysis of these passages is not included. Nonetheless, while there is certainly some truth to McFarlane's claims, one might be forgiven for thinking that he was not quite as impartial as he claimed.

Whatever one makes of McFarlane's portrait of Wyclif, he did at least seek to draw back the veil of Protestant (and Roman Catholic) myth and glimpse something of Wyclif on Wyclif's own terms. McFarlane's work set the stage for many of the developments in Wyclif studies in the second half of the twentieth century.

Joseph H. Dahmus, who at one point had trained to become a Roman Catholic priest,[31] was another scholar who sought to dismantle Wyclif's mythos. Dahmus demonstrated no sympathy whatsoever for Wyclif in his studies. He argued in one article that Wyclif was a negligent pluralist, since he failed to provide a vicar for his prebend at Aust in the year 1367.[32] This judgment has been found much too harsh by later scholarship, since vicars were not always easy to find, especially since Wyclif was at a distance and as prebendary had no obligation to provide pastoral care.[33] Dahmus' monograph, *The Prosecution of John*

31. Dahmus, "Obituary of Joseph H. Dahmus," 571.

32. Dahmus, "Wyclyf Was a Negligent Pluralist."

33. See Orme, "Wycliffe and the Prebend of Aust," where he concludes, "In the context of his own day, Wycliffe's tenure of the prebend of Aust was largely unexceptional and unexceptionable, and even the bishop appears to have thought that his fault deserved sequestration,

Wyclyf, published in 1952, went further. Dahmus explicitly set himself the task of countering Workman's biography, producing in his own words "an indispensable corrective to Workman's standard biography of Wyclif."[34] Reviews noted that he was not entirely successful in his endeavor, one reviewer writing that "Dahmus seems to have deliberately set out to discredit Wyclif and every scholar who has had any good to say about him. This book provides an interesting discussion, but such sweeping statements and such heaps of scorn for scholars of the stature of Workman, Trevelyan, and Pantin, should be taken with a bit of salt."[35] McFarlane was dismissive in his review of the book,[36] while S. Harrison Thomson raised serious doubts about Dahmus' conclusions in his much more thorough review, noting that "epithets directed at Workman's study, 'absurd,' 'prejudice,' warn the reader that the author might himself be guilty of a lack of objectivity."[37]

Other studies began to take more interest in Wyclif's philosophical works, such as J. A. Robson's study of the place of Wyclif's *Summa de ente* (Summa on being) within the context of fourteenth-century Oxford.[38] Robson's portrayal of Wyclif, much like McFarlane's and Dahmus', is not particularly flattering:

---

not deprivation. It is only when he is regarded as a paragon that the episode becomes a serious issue." (152).

34. Dahmus, *The Prosecution of John Wyclyf*, v.

35. Tatnall, Review of *The Prosecution of John Wyclyf*, 218.

36. McFarlane, Review of *The Prosecution of John Wyclyf*.

37. Thomson, Review of *The Prosecution*, 566.

38. Robson, *Wyclif and the Oxford Schools*.

> Discredited both as prophet of the Reformation
> and as scholastic, Wyclif's reputation has been
> greatly damaged; and recent historians have
> dwelt with measured severity, if not with relish,
> on the more obviously unattractive facets of his
> thought and character. Vanished is the picture
> of the Great Reformer; in his place stands an
> obstinate and rancorous pedagogue.[39]

That Robson believed this to be a true portrait is not in doubt, nor can it be doubted that he sought the truth about Wyclif's early career, which he saw as a complete unit, in one place speaking of "the achievement of a man who was in 1370, by general consent, the outstanding philosopher of his generation at Oxford."[40] One gets the impression that Robson was disappointed and saddened by Wyclif's later treatises, which Robson characterized as a tragedy.[41]

Other mid-century studies of Wyclif began to look more closely at his exegetical works. For instance, Beryl Smalley, a pioneer in the history of the study of the Bible in the Middle Ages, and Gustav Benrath looked at Wyclif's biblical commentaries, contained in the *Postilla in totam bibliam*, a much-understudied part of the reformer's work.[42] It was Smalley who proved beyond doubt that Wyclif had commented on the whole of Scripture in eight parts.[43] Benrath,

39. Robson, *Wyclif and the Oxford Schools*, 4.

40. Robson, *Wyclif and the Oxford Schools*, 17.

41. Robson, *Wyclif and the Oxford Schools*, 17.

42. Smalley, "John Wyclif's *Postilla*"; Benrath, *Wyclifs Bibelkommentar*.

43. Smalley, "John Wyclif's *Postilla*"; Smalley, "Wyclif's *Postilla* on the Old Testament."

working from the discoveries of Smalley, undertook an extensive study of the manuscripts of Wyclif's commentaries, editing several passages and analyzing both Wyclif's sources and his original thought, finding him to be thoroughly traditional and, as one reviewer noted, being disappointed at "how very far he was from Luther and more recent attitudes to Scripture."[44] Dom Paul de Vooght and Michael Hurley both studied Wyclif's hermeneutics, the former arguing that Wyclif interpreted Scripture with reference to patristic and later commentaries[45] and the latter arguing that Wyclif held a strict *sola scriptura* hermeneutic, which Hurley saw as creating a separation between Bible and Church, a rift that was ultimately destructive.[46] These authors, all Roman Catholic with the exception of the Lutheran Benrath, are representative of the turn toward an objective, detached historiography of Wyclif. By this point, the confessional agendas, while still present, had taken a backseat to what Wyclif actually thought and wrote, examined on his own terms in his own context. The arguments were no longer polemical, but scholarly. This move allowed the Roman Catholics de Vooght and Hurley to disagree fundamentally on the nature of Wyclif's hermeneutics; whereas earlier scholarship might have agreed on what Wyclif said and taught, disagreeing on the fundamental truth value of those teachings, modern scholarship at this

---

44. Wenzel, Review of *Wyclifs Bibelkommentar*, 122.

45. Vooght, *Les sources de la doctrine chrétienne*, 168–200; Vooght, "Wyclif et la *scriptura sola*."

46. Hurley, "Scriptura Sola."

period had different concerns. Thus, for example, Hurley could write, "I should like to think that in all this I have not been judging a fourteenth-century theologian according to twentieth-century categories, but have been faithful to the theological standpoint of his own time."[47] This is the sensibility of a modern, professional historian. Robson was right to say that the picture of the Great Reformer had vanished but a new portrait had begun to emerge, one of a late-medieval theologian.

47. Hurley, "Scriptura Sola," 351.

5

Contemporary Work on Wyclif

CONTEMPORARY WYCLIF SCHOLARSHIP HAS not only moved decidedly away from confessional considerations but has also moved beyond the work of the mid-twentieth-century scholars who sought, along with McFarlane, to remove the layers of Protestant varnish from Wyclif's reputation. The focus is now more than ever on what Wyclif actually wrote and on where the opinions expressed in his genuine works place him among, and in relation to, his contemporaries. Some major recent works on Wyclif will be surveyed here in order to identify important themes.

The Latter Half of the Twentieth Century

In the sixty-five years since the publication of McFarlane's book, there has been a decided shift in emphasis away from Wyclif as Morning Star to Wyclif as late-medieval philosopher and theologian. As was noted in the previous chapter, hero worship has long since been set aside, at least among the ranks of historians. Scholars, mostly (but not always) disconnected from confessional concerns, are now more intent on trying to elucidate objectively what Wyclif actually thought and wrote. This approach was evident already in much mid-twentieth-century scholarship, such as that of Roman Catholics Smalley and de Vooght and of the German Lutheran Benrath, as well as Margaret Aston, a student of McFarlane's who published extensively on heterodoxy and popular religion.[1]

The work of Michael Wilks, a historian of ideas, was fundamental to the shift that took place in Wyclif studies during the second half of the twentieth century. McFarlane's biography, the dominant scholarly view of Wyclif when Wilks started publishing in 1965, was based more on a reading of the chronicles of the time than on Wyclif's own writings. Over the span of thirty-five years, Wilks read and reread Wyclif's work and published a number of papers on him, especially for the Ecclesiastical History Society, with which he was actively involved, a scholarly society that was founded by the High Anglican Clifford Dugmore but had increasingly broader interests.[2] Wilks' interest was primarily in Wyclif's political ideas and political theology, attending to such questions as his theory of property, his ecclesiology, and the origins of Lollardy

1. Several seminal articles were gathered into two collections, *Lollards and Reformers* and *Faith and Fire*.

2. See Hudson, introduction to *Wyclif*, xi–xii. For a history of the society, which has had presidents from numerous denominational backgrounds, see Fletcher, "*A Very Agreeable Society*".

as a protest movement.[3] Writing at the turn of the twenty-first century, scholar Anne Hudson was of the opinion that "in some ways Wyclif studies have still not caught up with his expertise: there remain few if any with his command of Wyclif's writings, none who understand so much of the theoretical background to Wyclif's ecclesiological ideas."[4]

Anne Hudson has likewise studied Wyclif's life and works, and those of his followers, since the 1960s. Retired from Lady Margaret Hall, Oxford, in 2003, Hudson continues to publish on the transmission of Wyclif's works, on Middle English texts, and especially on the Middle English translation of the Latin Bible, usually referred to as the Wycliffite Bible.[5] Her *Premature Reformation: Wycliffite Texts and Lollard History*, published in 1988, was a watershed for the study of the Wycliffite reform movement. Turning to the evidence buried in manuscripts and the works of the Wycliffites themselves, Hudson in effect argued against the earlier interpretations of McFarlane and others, who thought that Wycliffism had petered out by the 1430s, and for a consistency and vitality in the Wycliffite movement even into the early sixteenth century.[6] By doing so, Hudson re-established, within modern scholarly limits, the influence of

3. See Wilks, "Predestination, Property, and Power"; Wilks, "Early Oxford Wyclif"; Wilks, "The Origins of Lollardy."

4. Hudson, introduction to *Wyclif*, xvi.

5. See the bibliography for a listing of Hudson's works related to Wyclif, his writings, and the Middle English Bible.

6. Hudson, *Premature Reformation*, 494–96.

Wyclif on reform in England, an idea precious to many Protestants, as previous chapters have demonstrated.

Hudson has done more, perhaps, than any other scholar to trace the movements and survival of Wyclif's works both in England and on the Continent. During the 1990s and into the first decades of the twenty-first century, she produced a series of publications demonstrating, among other conclusions, that Wyclif's works survive at about the same rate as other medieval works, despite the efforts of ecclesiastical authorities to eradicate his teachings,[7] and that the cross-referencing in his works, as useful as it might be for certain scholarly endeavors, has its limits in determining the order and dating of the reformer's corpus.[8] Other scholars have also advanced the scholarly community's knowledge of Wyclif's works as they are preserved in manuscript. Working from his father S. Harrison's notes begun in 1925, Williel R. Thomson published an indispensable guide to the known manuscripts of Wyclif's works in 1983, in time for the six-hundredth anniversary of Wyclif's death.[9] Textual studies and editions have continued intermittently since the Wyclif Society ceased publishing in 1922 and dissolved in 1924. Allen du Pont Breck published an edition of *De Trinitate* (On the Trinity) in 1967 with the University of Colorado Press,

7. See Hudson, *Studies in the Transmission of Wyclif's Writings.* For the conclusion about the survival rates of Wyclif's works, see also Hudson, "Books and their Survival," 225–44; Hudson, "The Survival of Wyclif's Works."

8. Hudson, "Cross-referencing in Wyclif's Latin Works."

9. Thomson, *The Latin Writings of John Wyclyf.*

and *De universalibus* (On Universals), edited by Ivan Mueller, was published by Oxford University Press in 1984 with an accompanying English translation by Anthony Kenny.

With the publication of *De universalibus*, historians of philosophy began to take a more active interest in Wyclif the philosopher, especially his realism. Kenny published a philosophical biography of Wyclif for the Oxford Past Masters series in 1985, and he edited a collection of important lectures delivered at Oxford in the 1984–1985 academic year, which appeared as *Wyclif in His Times* in 1986. The very title demonstrates the shift toward an emphasis on contextualization.

The sexcentenary of Wyclif's death in 1984 was connected with another such event, the possible seven-hundredth anniversary of William of Ockham's birth (1285), in the organization of an important conference under the auspices of the Ecclesiastical History Society at Queen's College, Oxford. This conference, yoking together two champions of opposing philosophical schools, resulted in the publication of *From Ockham to Wyclif*, edited by Wilks and Hudson. The collection included numerous groundbreaking studies based on close readings of Wyclif's works. Anthony Kenny, for example, basing his work on the recent edition and translation of the *De universalibus* that he helped produce, demonstrated that Wyclif's realism did not make him a determinist, at least not in the sense that he limited the freedom of human action.[10] Other studies looked at the influence of Robert Grosseteste on Wyclif's conception of hierarchy[11] or the expanded literal sense of his biblical interpretation.[12] These articles demonstrate quite clearly a trend that has been noted already, an increased specialization in Wyclif studies as scholars have turned to more technical aspects of Wyclif's thought and to textual matters relating to the extant manuscripts of his works.

The celebration of the sexcentenary of Wyclif's death thus witnessed a movement beyond the Protestant mythos of Wyclif the Morning Star of the Reformation. This was not, as it was in the mid-twentieth century, a simple rejection of any connection with the Reformation, but rather a beginning of the attempt to understand Wyclif not in terms of how later religious controversies worked out, but in terms of his own context as a late-fourteenth-century Oxford philosopher and theologian who taught a number of controversial ideas.

Wyclif Studies in the Twenty-First Century

In the twenty-first century, confessional concerns and party lines mean less than they ever have in the study of Wyclif and Lollardy. Two leading experts on Wyclif, the Episcopal priest Stephen Lahey and the lay Roman Catholic theologian and historian Ian Levy,

10. Kenny, "Realism and Determinism in the Early Wyclif."

11. Luscombe, "Wyclif and Hierarchy."

12. Evans, "Wyclif on Literal and Metaphorical."

have produced a number of complementary studies and even agree that Wyclif likely sent out something like the famed Poor Preachers.[13] The imperative for contemporary scholars is the recovery of Wyclif as late-medieval theologian and philosopher, with an emphasis on contextualization and, as Fiona Somerset once put it, "what Wyclif actually said."[14] This attitude has led scholarship beyond the traditional focuses of Wyclif the Bible translator and Wyclif the proto-Reformer and has opened up new avenues of inquiry; instead of rehashing old arguments about Wyclif's Protestantism, scholarship has begun to look at understudied aspects such as Wycliffite spirituality[15] and Wyclif's sermons and preaching program.[16]

Stephen Lahey has looked extensively at Wyclif's theory of *dominium*, first in his *Philosophy and Politics in the Thought of John Wyclif* (2003) and then in his intellectual biography of Wyclif for Oxford's Great Medieval Thinkers series, published in 2009. Ian Levy has written numerous technical studies of various aspects of Wyclif's theology, such as his rejection of transubstantiation and his understanding of Scripture.[17] He has also published an influential

13. Stephen E. Lahey, personal communication to Sean A. Otto, 7 August 2013.

14. Fiona Somerset, personal conversation with Sean A. Otto, May 2010.

15. See Hornbeck et al., *Wycliffite Spirituality*; Somerset, *Feeling Like Saints*.

16. See studies by Otto in the bibliography.

17. See the various studies by Stephen E. Lahey and by Ian Christopher Levy listed in the bibliography.

monograph on the interaction of these two aspects of Wyclif's thought.[18] Both men have published translations of Wyclif's works.[19] The two have also collaborated, as in what is probably the most important recent work on Wyclif, the collection of essays edited by Levy in 2006 and entitled *A Companion to John Wyclif: Late Medieval Theologian*. Both scholars exemplify current scholarly attitudes in Wyclif Studies in that they are concerned with accuracy in the portrayal of Wyclif and his thought and base their work on a rigorous examination of the primary sources.

Lahey and Levy are far from alone in their research. Specialized studies on Wyclif's philosophy and theology continue to appear regularly, and a more accurate, contextualized portrait of Wyclif has been emerging over the past forty years. There is still much to be learned about Wyclif, and there are several avenues for fruitful study.

18. Levy, *John Wyclif's Theology of the Eucharist*.

19. Lahey has translated the entire *Trialogus* as well as selections of the *De mandatis divinis* (On the divine commandments), the *Confessio*, "the Six Yokes," "Sermon 29," "On Love," and "On the Lord's Prayer." Levy has translated selections of *On the Truth of Holy Scripture*. See the bibliography for details.

6

Conclusion
The Future of Wyclif Studies

IF, AS THE EVIDENCE suggests, Wyclif studies have become post-confessional, and if the concern is now about what Wyclif actually wrote and the context in which he wrote it, there still remains much work to be done before the scholarly community can have as full an understanding of the man and his context as possible. Two kinds of contributions in particular ought to be mentioned: editorial work and possible thematic studies.

Editorial Work

The editorial work of the Wyclif Society was never fully completed. There are a few works, most importantly Wyclif's substantial biblical commentaries, that are still extant only in manuscript, and some other works, like Wyclif's *sanctorale* sermons and his major logical works, are in need of new editions. Wyclif's works, of course, are not unique in this, as there are hundreds of manuscripts of medieval sermons and tracts that could profitably be edited. The current academic climate is not friendly to these sorts of endeavors, however; many universities do not count this sort of work for tenure review, and of course, tenure itself is becoming rarer and rarer. Nonetheless, some of this editorial work is already underway. An edition of Wyclif's *De scientia Dei* (On God's knowledge), part of Wyclif's *Summa de ente* (Summa on being), has recently been published by Luigi Campi, while editions of other works, such as the *De ideis* (On ideas), are in progress.

The fact that this work still remains to be done almost a hundred and fifty years after the founding of the Wyclif Society is remarkable and goes to show the importance of a strong and determined personality such as F. J. Furnivall to this type of work. It is to be hoped that the remaining writings that are extant only in manuscript, especially the biblical commentaries, and those works in need of updated critical editions will find editors willing to take up the task.

Themes

Apart from this editorial work, although often intimately linked with it, there is still much that can be learned from actually reading Wyclif's writings, even if the current editions are deficient or one has to do the painstaking work of consulting the manuscripts. Little attention has been paid, for example, to Wyclif's sermons, and this has led to a superficial understanding of Wyclif's theology of preaching; scholars have noted preaching's importance to Wyclif, but neither his sermons' contents nor the sermons' place in his program for grassroots reform have been studied in any great detail. The interconnections between the biblical commentaries and the sermons, recognized since Benrath's study in the 1960s, is an area that could be explored in greater detail and quite profitably if ever an edition of the commentaries were to be produced.

Comparatively little has been done to study the pastoral aspects of Wyclif's thought, as scholarly attention has been captivated by the more controversial and polemical treatises as well as his philosophical works. Wyclif is often characterized as gruff and curmudgeonly, as a self-assured and even cocky philosopher who was led to reforming positions by his philosophical beliefs or by his strident biblicism. He could certainly be abrasive, and the pastoral aspect of his work, the great care that he had for the souls of the faithful, is often obscured by his frequent venting of spleen, but a more thorough and careful look at his pastoral theology, something that has only recently started to gain scholarly interest, deserves further investigation.[1]

The opening up of former Soviet territories in the 1990s, especially the Czech lands, has led to an increase in fruitful interchanges between Western European, North American, and Eastern European scholars and has made important manuscript

---

1. See, e.g., Hornbeck et al., *Wycliffite Spirituality*.

resources accessible. The link between Wyclif and the Hussites has been acknowledged since the very beginning, but a more nuanced understanding, free of Protestant and Roman Catholic polemics, has been slow in materializing. One can only hope that such scholarly interchange will continue and that a more nuanced and complete portrait of the links between Wyclif's thought and the Bohemian reform movement will emerge, especially in the West.

Conclusion

Wyclif has been a controversial figure since his own time, often dividing opinion between devoted followers and intransigent opponents. In the fifteenth and sixteenth centuries, there was already a developing mythos about him, and he was variously used as a symbol of heretical depravity or of valorous defense of the Gospel. The Reformation calcified opinions, and the two subsequent centuries did not see much development. The nineteenth century marked the beginning of important changes in scholarly opinion, with confessional approaches weakening and giving way to greater objectivity. This trend was strengthened by the emergence of a professional class of historians around the turn of the twentieth century, but the established confessional biases were not quickly done away with; for example, founders of the evangelical Wycliffe College in Toronto and the men the College trained for ministry, with their confessional tendencies, were among the movers and shakers of Ontario society well into the twentieth century. Finally, in the postwar period, the remaining confessional bias was successfully removed from professional historians' contributions to Wyclif studies, as seen in works like those of McFarlane. Today, confessional mythmaking is gone, even, it can be argued, from the ranks of Church historians at seminaries; the goal is no longer to show why one particular branch of Christianity is correct, but to present as accurate a picture as possible of the past. This is not to say, of course, that past historians, with their confessional concerns, were being dishonest; rather, their motivations occasionally led them to make mistakes, as happens with all people. Finally, as the concerns of the twentieth century give way to those of the twenty-first, it is encouraging that there are still new things to be learned about the past, new ways of seeing and engaging, even with figures so well studied as Wyclif.

)

Bibliography

Articles of Religion. In *The Book of Common Prayer* [. . .] *according to the Use of the Anglican Church of Canada* [. . .], 698–714. Toronto: Anglican Book Centre, 1962.

Aston, Margaret. *Faith and Fire: Popular and Unpopular Religion, 1350–1600.* London: Hambledon, 1993.

———. "John Wycliffe's Reformation Reputation." *Past & Present* 30 (1964) 23–51.

———. *Lollards and Reformers: Images and Literacy in Late Medieval Religion.* London: Hambledon, 1984.

———. "Lollardy and Sedition, 1381–1431." *Past & Present* 17 (1960) 1–44.

Aylmer, John. *An Harborowe for Faithfull and Trewe Subiectes.* Strasborow [but *recte* London]: n.p., 1559. Quoted in Patrick Collinson, "Thomas Cranmer," in *The English Religious Tradition and the Genius of Anglicanism*, edited by Geoffrey Rowell, 79–104. Oxford: Ikon, 1992.

Bale, John. *Illustrium maioris Britanniae scriptorum* [. . .] *summarium.* N.p.: n.p., 1548. Quoted in translation in Margaret Aston, "John Wycliffe's Reformation Reputation." *Past & Present* 30 (1964) 23–51.

Benrath, Gustav Adolf. *Wyclifs Bibelkommentar.* Berlin: de Gruyter, 1966.

Bose, Mishtooni. "The Opponents of John Wyclif." In *A Companion to John Wyclif: Late Medieval Theologian*, edited by Ian Christopher Levy, 407–55. Leiden: Brill, 2006.

Buddenseig, Rudolph. Introduction to *Polemical Works in Latin.* 2 vols., I:i–c. London: Trübner, 1883. Quoted in H. L. Spencer, "F. J. Furnivall's Last Fling: The Wyclif Society and Anglo-German

Scholarly Relations, 1882–1922." *Review of English Studies* 65 (2014) 790–811.

Burgess, Clive. "A Hotbed of Heresy? Fifteenth-Century Bristol and Lollardy Reconsidered." In *The Fifteenth Century III: Authority and Subversion*, edited by Linda Clark, 43–62. Woodbridge: Boydell, 2003.

Burrows, Montagu. *Wiclif's Place in History*. London: William Isbister, 1884.

Collinson, Patrick. "Thomas Cranmer." In *The English Religious Tradition and the Genius of Anglicanism*, edited by Geoffrey Rowell, 79–104. Oxford: Ikon, 1992.

Copeland, Rita. "William Thorpe and His Lollard Community: Intellectual Labour and the Representation of Dissent." In *Bodies and Disciplines: Intersections of Literature and History in Fifteenth-Century England*, edited by Barbara A. Hanawalt and David Wallace, 199–221. London: University of Minnesota Press, 1996.

Copsey, Richard. "Thomas Netter of Walden: A Biography." In *Thomas Netter of Walden: Carmelite, Diplomat and Theologian (c.1372–1430)*, edited by Johan Bergström-Allen and Richard Copsey, 23–111. Faversham, UK: St. Albert's Press, 2009.

Dahmus, Joseph H. *The Prosecution of John Wyclyf*. New Haven: Yale University Press, 1952.

———. "Wyclyf Was a Negligent Pluralist." *Speculum* 28 (1953) 378–81.

Dahmus, John W. "Obituary of Joseph H. Dahmus." *Catholic Historical Review* 91 (2005) 572–73.

Evans, G. R. "Wyclif on Literal and Metaphorical." In *From Ockham to Wyclif*, edited by Anne Hudson and Michael Wilks, 259–66. Studies in Church History Subsidia 5. Oxford: Blackwell, 1987.

Fletcher, Stella. "*A Very Agreeable Society*": The Ecclesiastical History Society, 1961–2011. Warrington, UK: Ecclesiastical History Society, 2011.

Friesen, Abraham. "Medieval Heretics or Forerunners of the Reformation: The Protestant Rewriting of the History of Medieval Heresy." In *The Devil, Heresy and Witchcraft in the Middle Ages: Essays in Honour of Jeffery B. Russell*, edited by Alberto Ferreiro, 165–89. Leiden: Brill, 1998.

Gasquet, Francis. *The Old English Bible and Other Studies*. London: John C. Nimmo, 1897. Second Edition, London: George Bell, 1908.

———. "The Pre-Reformation English Bible." *Dublin Review* 115 (1894) 122–52.

Hague, Dyson. *The Life and Work of John Wycliffe*. London: Church Book Room, 1935.

Harmon, Nolan B., ed. *The Encyclopedia of World Methodism*. Nashville: United Methodist Publishing House, 1974.

Hilton, Rodney. *Bond Men Made Free: Medieval Peasant Movements and the English Rising of 1381*. New York: Routledge, 1973.

Hornbeck, J. Patrick II. *What Is a Lollard? Dissent and Belief in Late Medieval England*. Oxford: Oxford University Press, 2010.

Hornbeck, J. Patrick II, Stephen E. Lahey, and Fiona Somerset, eds. and trans. *Wycliffite Spirituality*. New York: Paulist Press, 2013.

Hudson, Anne. "Aspects of the 'Publication' of Wyclif's Latin Sermons." In *Late-Medieval Religious Texts and their Transmission: Essays in Honour of A. I. Doyle*, edited by Alistar J. Minnis, 121–30. Woodbridge, UK: Brewer, 1994.

———. "Books and Their Survival: The Case of English Manuscripts of Wyclif's Latin Works." *Viator* (2011) 225–44.

———. "Cross–referencing in Wyclif's Latin Works." In *The Medieval Church: Universities, Heresy, and the Religious Life*, edited by Peter Biller and Barrie Dobson, 193–215. Studies in Church History Subsidia 11. Woodbridge: Boydell, 1999. Reprint, in *Studies in the Transmission of Wyclif's Writings*, by Anne Hudson, Item IV. Aldershot, UK: Variorum, 2008.

———. "Dangerous Fictions: Indulgences in the Thought of Wyclif and His Followers." In *Promissory Notes on the Treasury of Merits: Indulgences in Late Medieval Europe*, edited by R. N. Swanson, 197–214. Leiden: Brill, 2007.

———. "From Oxford to Prague: The Writings of John Wyclif and His English Followers in Bohemia." *Slavonic and East European Review* 75 (1997) 642–57. Reprint, in *Studies in the Transmission of Wyclif's Writings*, by Anne Hudson, Item II. Aldershot, UK: Variorum, 2008.

———. Introduction to *Wycliffe: Political Ideas and Practice*, by Michael Wilks, xi–xvi. Oxford: Oxbow, 2000.

———. "The Lay Folk's Catechism: A Postscript." *Viator* 19 (1988) 307–10.

———. "A Lollard Compilation and the Dissemination of Wycliffite Thought." *Journal of Theological Studies* 23 (1972) 65–81.

———. "Some Aspects of Lollard Book Production." In *Schism, Heresy, and Religious Protest*, edited by Derek Baker, 147–57. Studies in Church History 9. Cambridge: Cambridge University Press, 1972.

———. "Lollardy: The English Heresy?" In *Religion and National Identity*, edited by Stuart Mews, 261–83. Studies in Church History 18. Oxford: Blackwell, 1982.

———. "A New Look at the Lay Folk's Catechism." *Viator* 16 (1985) 243–58.

———. "Notes of an Early Fifteenth-Century Research Assistant, and the Emergence of the 267 Articles against Wyclif." *English Historical Review* 118 (2003) 685–97.

———. "Poor Preachers, Poor Men: Views of Poverty in Wyclif and His Followers." In *Haeresie und Vorzeitige Reformation in Spätmittelalter*, edited by F. Smahel, 41–53. Munich: Oldenbourg, 1998.

———. *The Premature Reformation: Wycliffite Texts and Lollard History*. Oxford: Oxford University Press, 1988.

———, ed. *Selections from English Wycliffite Writings*. Cambridge: Cambridge University Press, 1978.

———. "So Far and Yet So Near." In *Preaching the Word in Manuscript and in Print in Late Medieval England: Essays in Honour of Susan Powell*, edited by Martha W. Driver and Veronica O'Mara, 49–62. Turnhout, Belgium: Brepols, 2013.

———. *Studies in the Transmission of Wyclif's Writings*. Aldershot, UK: Variorum, 2008.

———. "The Survival of Wyclif's Works in England and Bohemia." In *Studies in the Transmission of Wyclif's Writings*, by Anne Hudson, Item XVI, 1–43. Aldershot, UK: Variorum, 2008.

———. "Thomas Netter's *Doctrinale* and the Lollards." In *Thomas Netter of Walden: Carmelite, Diplomat and Theologian (c.1372–1430)*, edited by Johan Bergström-Allen and Richard Copsey, 179–97. Faversham, UK: St. Albert's Press, 2009.

———. "Wyclif and the English Language." In *Wyclif in His Times*, edited by Anthony Kenny, 85–103. Oxford: Clarendon, 1986.

———. "Wyclif's Books." In *Image, Text, and Church, 1380–1600: Essays for Margaret Aston*, edited by Linda Clark et al., 8–36. Toronto: Pontifical Institute of Medieval Studies, 2009.

———. "Wyclif's Latin Sermons: Questions of Form, Date and Audience." *Archives d'histoire er littéraire du moyen âge* 68 (2001) 223–48. Reprint, in *Studies in the Transmission of Wyclif's Writings*, by Anne Hudson, Item VI. Aldershot, UK: Variorum, 2008.

———. "Wycliffism at Oxford, 1381–1411." In *Wyclif in His Times*, edited by Anthony Kenny, 67–84. Oxford: Clarendon, 1986.

———. "A Wycliffite Scholar of the Early Fifteenth Century." In *The Bible in the Medieval World*, edited by Katherine Walsh and

Diana Woods, 301–15. Studies in Church History Subsidia 4. Oxford: Blackwell, 1985.

Hurley, Michael. "'Scriptura Sola': Wyclif and His Critics." *Traditio* 16 (1960) 275–352.

Keen, Maurice. "The Influence of Wyclif." In *Wyclif in His Times*, edited by Anthony Kenny, 127–45. Oxford: Clarendon, 1986.

Kelly, Henry Ansgar. *The Middle English Bible: A Reassessment.* Philadelphia: University of Pennsylvania Press, 2016.

Kenny, Anthony. "The Accursed Memory: The Counter-Reformation Reputation of John Wyclif." In *Wyclif in His Times*, edited by Anthony Kenny, 147–68. Oxford: Clarendon, 1986.

———. "Realism and Determinism in the Early Wyclif." In *From Ockham to Wyclif*, edited by Anne Hudson and Michael Wilks, 165–78. Studies in Church History Subsidia 5. Oxford: Blackwell, 1987.

———. *Wyclif.* Oxford: Oxford University Press, 1985.

Kern, Anton. "Loserth, Johann (1846–1936)." *Global Anabaptist Mennonite Encyclopedia Online,* http://www.gameo.org/encyclopedia/contents/loserth_johann_1846_1936.

King, John N. *English Reformation Literature: The Tudor Origins of the Protestant Tradition.* Princeton: Princeton University Press, 1982.

Knapp, Peggy Ann. "John Wyclif as Bible Translator: The Texts for the English Sermons." *Speculum* 46 (1971) 713–20.

———. *The Style of John Wyclif's English Sermons.* The Hague: Mouton, 1977.

Kras, P. "Wyclif's Tradition in Fifteenth Century Poland: The Heresy of Andrej Gal'ka of Dobcyzn." *Bohemian Reformation and Religious Practice* 5 (2002) 191–210.

Kretzmann, Norman, et al., eds. *The Cambridge History of Later Medieval Philosophy.* Cambridge: Cambridge University Press, 1982.

———. "Continua, Indivisibles, and Change in Wyclif's Logic of Scripture." In *Wyclif in His Times*, edited by Anthony Kenny, 31–65. Oxford: Clarendon, 1986.

Kühn-Steinhausen, H. "Wyclif-Handschriften in Deutschland." *Zentralblatt für Bibliothekswesen* 47 (1930) 625–27.

Lahey, Stephen E. *John Wyclif.* Oxford: Oxford University Press, 2009.

———. "Of Divine Ideas and Insolubles: Wyclif's Explanation of God's Understanding of Sin." *Modern Schoolman* 86 (2009) 211–32.

———. *Philosophy and Politics in the Thought of John Wyclif.* Cambridge: Cambridge University Press, 2003.

———. "Richard Fitzralph and John Wyclif: Untangling Armachanus from the Wycliffites." In *Richard Fitzralph: Life and Thought*, edited by Michael Dunne and Simon Nolan, 204–13. Dublin: Four Courts Press, 2013.

———. Introduction to *Trialogus*, by John Wyclif, translated by Stephen E. Lahey, 1–37. Cambridge: Cambridge University Press, 2013.

———. "Wyclif and Lollardy." In *The Medieval Theologians*, edited by G. R. Evans, 334–54. Malden, MA: Blackwell, 2001.

———. "Wyclif and Rights." *Journal of the History of Ideas* 58 (1997) 1–20.

———. "Wyclif and Toleration." In *Difference and Dissent*, edited by John C. Laursen and Cary J. Nederman, 39–66. New York: Rowman & Littlefield, 1997.

———. "Wyclif, the 'Hussite Philosophy,' and the Law of Christ." *Bohemian Reformation and Religious Practice* 9 (2014) 54–71.

———. "Wyclif's Trinitarian and Christological Theology." In *A Companion to John Wyclif: Late Medieval Theologian*, edited by Ian Christopher Levy, 127–98. Leiden: Brill, 2006.

Lechler, Gotthard. *Johann von Wiclif und die Vorgeschichte der Reformation*. 2 vols. Leipzig: Friedrich Fleischer, 1873.

———. *John Wycliffe and His English Precursors*. Edited and translated by Peter Lorimer. London: Religious Tract Society, 1884.

Levy, F. J. "The Reformation and English History Writing." In *Tudor Historical Thought*, 79–123. Toronto: University of Toronto Press, 2004.

Levy, Ian Christopher. "*Christus qui mentiri non potest*: John Wyclif's Rejection of Transubstantiation." *Recherches de théologie et philosophie médiévales* 66 (1999) 316–34.

———, ed. *A Companion to John Wyclif: Late Medieval Theologian*. Leiden: Brill, 2006.

———. "Defining the Responsibility of the Late Medieval Theologian: The Debate between John Kynnyngham and John Wyclif." *Carmelus* 19 (2002) fasc. 1:5–29.

———. "Dispensing against the Apostle: John Wyclif and the Canonists." In *Inventing Modernity in Medieval European Thought, ca. 1100–ca. 1550*, edited by Bettina Koch and Cary Nederman, 213–29. Berlin: Medieval Institute, 2019.

———. "The Fight for the Sacred Sense in Late Medieval England." *Anglican Theological Review* 85 (2003) 165–76.

———. "Grace and Freedom in the Soteriology of John Wyclif." *Traditio* 60 (2005) 279–337.

———. "John Wyclif and Augustinian Realism." *Augustiniana* 48 (1998) 87–106.

———. "John Wyclif and Christian Humanism." In *Medieval Christian Humanism*, edited by John Bequette, 297–312. Leiden: Brill, 2016.

———. "John Wyclif and the Primitive Papacy." *Viator* 38 (2007) 159–89.

———. "John Wyclif: Christian Patience in a Time of War." *Theological Studies* 66 (2005) 330–57.

———. "John Wyclif on Papal Election, Correction, and Deposition." *Mediaeval Studies* 69 (2007) 141–85.

———. "John Wyclif's Neo-Platonic View of Scripture in Its Christological Context." *Medieval Philosophy and Theology* 11 (2003) 227–40.

———. *John Wyclif's Theology of the Eucharist in Its Medieval Context*. Rev. and exp. ed. of *Scriptural Logic, Real Presence, and the Parameters of Orthodoxy*. Milwaukee: Marquette, 2014.

———. *Holy Scripture and the Quest for Authority at the End of the Middle Ages*. Notre Dame, IN: University of Notre Dame Press, 2012.

———. "The Place of Holy Scripture in John Wyclif's Theology." In *The Wycliffite Bible: Origin, History and Interpretation*, edited by Elizabeth Solopova, 27–48. Leiden: Brill, 2017.

———. "Texts for a Poor Church: John Wyclif and the Decretals." *Essays in Medieval Studies* 20 (2004) 94–107.

———. "Thomas Netter on the Eucharist." In *Thomas Netter of Walden: Carmelite, Diplomat and Theologian (c.1372–1430)*, edited by Johan Bergström-Allen and Richard Copsey, 273–314. Faversham, UK: St. Albert's Press, 2009.

———. "Useful Foils: Lessons Learned from Jews in John Wyclif's Call for Church Reform." *Medieval Encounters* 7 (2001) 125–45.

———. Was John Wyclif's Theology of the Eucharist Donatistic?" *Scottish Journal of Theology* 53 (2000) 137–53.

———. "Wyclif Contextualized—Magister Sacrae Paginae." In *Wycliffite Controversies*, edited by Mishtooni Bose and J. Patrick Hornbeck II, 33–57. Turnhout, Belgium: Brepols, 2011.

Lewis, John. *The History of the Life and Sufferings of the Reverend and Learned John Wicliffe, D. D.* London: Robert Knaplock, 1720.

Loserth, Johann. *Hus und Wicklif: Zur Genesis der Husitischen Lehre*. Prague: F. Tempsky, 1884.

Luscombe, David. "Wyclif and Hierarchy." In *From Ockham to Wyclif*, edited by Anne Hudson and Michael Wilks, 233–44. Oxford: Blackwell, 1987.

Lytle, Guy Fitch. "John Wyclif, Martin Luther and Edward Powell: Heresy and the Oxford Theology Faculty at the Beginning of the Reformation." In *From Ockham to Wyclif*, edited by Anne Hudson and Michael Wilks, 465–80. Oxford: Blackwell, 1987.

McFarlane, K. B. *John Wycliffe and the Beginnings of English Nonconformity*. Harmondsworth: Penguin, 1972.

———. Review of *The Prosecution of John Wyclyf*, by Joseph H. Dahmus. *Annals of the American Academy of Political and Social Science* 288 (1953) 197.

Mudroch, Vaclav. *The Wyclyf Tradition*. Edited by Albert Compton Reeves. Athens, OH: Ohio University Press, 1979.

Mullins, Patrick. "Netter's Defence of Extreme Unction against Wyclif." In *Thomas Netter of Walden: Carmelite, Diplomat and Theologian (c.1372–1430)*, edited by Johan Bergström-Allen and Richard Copsey, 251–70. Faversham, UK: St. Albert's Press, 2009.

Nolcken, Christina von. "Another Kind of Saint: A Lollard Perspective of John Wyclif." In *From Ockham to Wyclif*, edited by Anne Hudson and Michael Wilks, 429–44. Studies in Church History Subsidia 5. Oxford: Blackwell, 1987.

O'Donnell, Christopher. "A Controversy on Confirmation: Thomas Netter of Walden and Wyclif." In *Thomas Netter of Walden: Carmelite, Diplomat and Theologian (c.1372–1430)*, edited by Johan Bergström-Allen and Richard Copsey, 317–32. Faversham, UK: St. Albert's Press, 2009.

Orme, Nicholas. "John Wycliffe and the Prebend of Aust." *Journal of Ecclesiastical History* 61.1 (2010): 144–52.

Otto, Sean A. "The Authority of the Preacher in a Sermon of John Wyclif." *Mirator* 12 (2011) 77–93.

———. "The Contrition of Mary Magdalene: John Wyclif and the Preaching of Penance." In *From Learning to Love: Schools, Law, and Pastoral Care in the Middle Ages; Essays in Honour of Joseph W. Goering*, edited by Tristan Sharp et al., 718–34. Toronto: PIMS, 2017.

———. "John Wyclif and Thomas Cranmer on Penance." In *Change and Transformation: Essays in Anglican History*, edited by Thomas P. Power, 1–23. Eugene, OR: Wipf & Stock, 2013.

———. "The Perils of the Flesh: John Wyclif's Preaching on the Five Bodily Senses." In *The Five Senses in Medieval and Early Modern England*, edited by Annette Kern-Staehler et al., 163–76. Intersections 44. Leiden: Brill, 2016.

————. "Predestination and the Two Cities: The Authority of Augustine and the Nature of the Church in Giles of Rome and John Wyclif." In *Authorities in the Middle Ages: Influence, Legitimacy and Power in Medieval Society*, edited by Tuija Ainonen et al., 145–58. Berlin: de Gruyter, 2013.

————. "The Reform Program of John Wyclif's Latin Sermons." In *Reformation Worlds: Antecedents and Legacies in the Anglican Tradition*, edited by Sean A. Otto and Thomas P. Power, 43–59. New York: Peter Lang, 2016.

————. "The Word of God Is Seed: John Wyclif's Evangelical Theology and the Naming of Wycliffe College." In *A Flight of Parsons: The Divinity Diaspora of Trinity College Dublin*, edited by Thomas P. Power, 300–317. Eugene, OR: Wipf & Stock, 2018.

Oxford Dictionary of National Biography. Edited by H. C. G. Matthew and Brian Harrison. Oxford: Oxford University Press, 2004.

Patchovsky, Alexander. "Heresy and Society: On the Political Function of Heresy in the Medieval World." In *Texts and Repression of Medieval Heresy*, edited by Caterina Bruschi and Peter Biller, 23–41. Woodbridge: York Medieval, 2003.

Robson, J. A. *Wyclif and the Oxford Schools: The Relation of the "Summa De Ente" to Scholastic Debates at Oxford in the Later Fourteenth Century*. Cambridge: Cambridge University Press, 1961.

Šmahel, František, and Ota Pavlicek, eds. *A Companion to Jan Hus*. Leiden: Brill, 2015.

Smalley, Beryl. "John Wyclif's *Postilla Super Totam Bibliam*." *Bodleian Library Record* 5 (1953) 186–205.

————. "Wyclif's *Postilla* on the Old Testament and His *Principium*." In *Oxford Studies Presented to Daniel Callus*, 253–96. Oxford: Clarendon, 1964.

Somerset, Fiona. *Feeling Like Saints: Lollard Writings after Wyclif*. Ithaca, NY: Cornell University Press, 2014.

————. "Their Writings." In *A Companion to Lollardy*, edited by J. Patrick Hornbeck II, 76–104. Leiden: Brill, 2016.

Spencer, H. L. "F. J. Furnivall's Last Fling: The Wyclif Society and Anglo-German Scholarly Relations, 1882–1922." *Review of English Studies* 65 (2014) 790–811.

Strohm, Paul. *England's Empty Throne: Usurpation and the Language of Legitimation, 1399–1422*. Philadelphia: University of Pennsylvania Press, 1998.

Tatnall, Edith. Review of *The Prosecution of John Wyclyf*, by Joseph H. Dahmus. *Church History* 40 (1972) 218.

Thomson, S. Harrison. Review of *The Prosecution of John Wyclyf*, by Joseph H. Dahmus. *Speculum* 28 (1953) 563–66.

Thomson, Williell R. *The Latin Writings of John Wyclyf: An Annotated Catalog*. Toronto: Pontifical Institute of Medieval Studies, 1983.

Van Dussen, Michael. *From England to Bohemia*. Cambridge: Cambridge University Press, 2012.

Vaughan, Robert. *John de Wycliffe, DD: A Monograph*. London: Seeley, 1853.

———. *The Life and Opinions of John Wycliffe, D.D.* 2 vols. London: Holdsworth & Ball, 1831.

Vooght, Paul de. *Les Sources de la doctrine chrétienne d'après les théologiens de XIVe siècle et du début du XVe siècle*. Paris: Desclée, 1954.

———. "Wyclif et la *scriptura sola*." *Ephemerides Theologicas Lovanienses* 39 (1963) 50–86.

Walsh, Katherine. "Wyclif's Legacy in Central Europe in the Late Fourteenth and Early Fifteenth Centuries." In *From Ockham to Wyclif*, edited by Anne Hudson and Michael Wilks, 397–417. Studies in Church History Subsidia 5. Oxford: Blackwell, 1987.

Wenzel, Siegfried. Review of *Wyclifs Bibelkommentar*, by Gustav A. Benrath. *Speculum* 43 (1968) 121–23.

Wilks, Michael. "The Early Oxford Wyclif: Papalist or Nominalist?" In *Wyclif: Political Ideas and Practice*, 33–62. Oxford: Oxbow, 2000.

———. "Royal Priesthood: The Origins of Lollardy." In *Wyclif: Political Ideas and Practice*, 101–16. Oxford: Oxbow, 2000.

———. "Predestination, Property, and Power: Wyclif's Theory of Dominion and Grace." In *Wyclif: Political Ideas and Practice*, 16–32. Oxford: Oxbow, 2000.

———. "Roman Candle or Damned Squib: The English Crusade of 1383." In *Wyclif: Political Ideas and Practice*, 253–72. Oxford: Oxbow, 2000.

———. *Wyclif: Political Ideas and Practice*. Oxford: Oxbow, 2000.

Workman, Herbert B. *John Wyclif: A Study of the English Medieval Church*. 2 vols. Oxford: Clarendon, 1926. Reprint, Eugene, OR: Wipf & Stock, 2001.

Wright, Donald. *The Professionalization of History in English Canada*. Toronto: University of Toronto Press, 2005.

Wrong, George M. *The Crusade of 1383: Known as That of the Bishop of Norwich*. London: James Parker, 1892.

———. *Historical Study in the University: An Inaugural Lecture*. Toronto: Bryant Press, 1895. Quoted in *The Professionalization of History in English Canada* by Donald Wright, 31. Toronto: University of Toronto Press, 2005.

Wyclif, John. "On Love." Edited and translated by Stephen E. Lahey. In *Wycliffite Spirituality*, edited and translated by J. Patrick Hornbeck II et al., 84–87. New York: Paulist, 2013.

———. "On the Divine Commandments (Selections)." Edited and translated by Stephen E. Lahey. In *Wycliffite Spirituality*, edited and translated by J. Patrick Hornbeck II et al., 87–146. New York: Paulist, 2013.

———. "On the Lord's Prayer." Edited and translated by Stephen E. Lahey. In *Wycliffite Spirituality*, edited and translated by J. Patrick Hornbeck II et al., 146–55. New York: Paulist, 2013.

———. *On the Truth of Holy Scripture*. Translated by Ian Christopher Levy. Kalamazoo, MI: Medieval Institute Publications, 2001.

———. *Opera minora*. Edited by Johan Loserth and F. D. Matthews. London: Trübner, 1913. Reprint, New York: Johnson Reprints, 1966.

———. "Sermon 29." Edited and translated by Stephen E. Lahey. In *Wycliffite Spirituality*, edited and translated by J. Patrick Hornbeck II et al., 63–71. New York: Paulist, 2013.

———. "The Six Yokes." Edited and translated by Stephen E. Lahey. In *Wycliffite Spirituality*, edited and translated by J. Patrick Hornbeck II et al., 71–84. New York: Paulist, 2013.

———. *Trialogus*. Edited by Gotthard Lechler. Oxford: Clarendon, 1869.

———. *Trialogus*. Edited and translated by Stephen E. Lahey. Cambridge: Cambridge University Press, 2013.